MIRANDA v. ARIZONA

Miranda
v. Arizona

"YOU HAVE THE RIGHT
TO REMAIN SILENT. . ."

by
Paul B. Wice

Historic Supreme Court Cases
FRANKLIN WATTS
A Division of Grolier Publishing
New York London Hong Kong Sydney
Danbury, Connecticut

345.7305

22.00

10/96

B. & T.

Photographs copyright ©: Research Division, Arizona Department of Library Archives and Public Records, Phoenix: pp. 12, 16, 25, 83, 109; Collection of the Supreme Court of the United States, Office of the Curator: pp. 32, 47, 62, 126 (Bob Oakes, National Geographic Society); Courtesy, Arizona Historical Society, Tucson: p. 35; The Bettmann Archive: pp. 41, 43; UPI/Bettmann: pp. 72, 75, 106, 112, 143; Archives of the Race Relations Department, United Church Board for Homeland Ministries, Amistad Research Center: p. 85; Collection, The Supreme Court Historical Society: pp. 93, 100; AP/ Wide World Photos: pp. 103, 134.

Library of Congress Cataloging-in-Publication Data

Wice, Paul B.
    Miranda v. Arizona: "You have the right to remain silent. . ." / Paul B. Wice
        p. cm — (Historic Supreme Court cases)
    Includes bibliographical references and index.
    ISBN 0-531-11250-0
    1. Miranda, Ernesto—Trials, litigation, etc.—Juvenile literature. 2. Trials (Rape)—Arizona—Juvenile literature. 3. Self-incrimination—United States—Juvenile literature. 4. Right to counsel—United States—Juvenile literature. 5. Police questioning—United States—Juvenile literature. I. Title II. Series.
KF224.M54W53 1996
345.73'056—dc20
                                                                            95-45284
[347.30556]   CIP

CONTENTS

MIRANDA v. ARIZONA

Chapter 1

A CONFESSION

After finishing work at the refreshment stand at the Paramount Theater in downtown Phoenix, Arizona, Lois Ann Jameson (not her real name) took a bus to Seventh and Marlette streets in the city's northeast section. She stepped off the bus a few minutes past midnight and began walking toward her home on Citrus Way. A car suddenly pulled out of a driveway, blocking her path. The driver got out of the vehicle. He walked alongside Jameson and then grabbed her and dragged her into the back of his car. Tying the woman's hands and ankles, the man warned her not to move. She felt a cold sharp object against her neck.

The man drove the car for twenty minutes before pulling to a stop in an outlying desert area. He ordered Jameson to remove all of her clothes. He then raped the young woman, took four dollars from her purse, allowed her to get dressed, and returned her to the neighborhood where he had abducted her.

Although stunned by the attack, Jameson walked about four blocks to her home, where she lived with her mother, sister, and brother-in-law. After bringing herself under control, she called the Phoenix Metro Police, and an officer quickly arrived on the scene. She related the kidnapping and rape, and the policeman took her to a local hospital to be examined. There, she described her assailant and his car to two other officers. The following day— Monday, March 4, 1963—Detective Carroll Cooley came to Jameson's home and spoke with her sister. He returned the next day to speak with Jameson and to ask more detailed questions about her abduction and rape. Her statements were still somewhat vague and inconsistent. In addition to her shyness and reluctance to talk about the attack, Jameson had a low IQ—that of about a thirteen-year-old. She had dropped out of school after years of failure.

Following the incident, with the police unable to piece together much of a case, Jameson returned to her job. Each night her brother-in-law met her at the bus stop and walked her home. On March 11, Jameson's brother-in-law spotted a car that he had noticed cruising the neighborhood recently. The 1953 Packard, with the letters DFL as part of its license plate number, roughly matched Jameson's description of the car driven by her attacker. Detectives ran a check and discovered the car was registered to Twila Hoffman, who lived in the nearby suburb of Mesa.

Detectives Carroll Cooley and Wilfred Young drove out to Mesa the following morning but found no one was at Hoffman's home. They did learn, however, that Hoffman and her boyfriend, Ernest Miranda, had moved two days earlier. Talking with neighbors, they discovered that Miranda roughly fit the description of Jameson's assailant. Upon learning that Miranda worked for United Produce, they were able to confirm that he was a night dockworker but had been off the night of March 3. Encouraged by this information, the detectives next went to the post office and found out that Miranda and Hoffman had moved to 2525 Mariposa. They also checked Mesa police records and learned that Miranda had a rather lengthy criminal record.

THE INTERROGATION

Cooley and Young returned to 2525 Mariposa at 8:30 A.M., shortly after Miranda had returned from work. They observed a 1953 Packard parked in the driveway. The detectives knocked on the door, and Twila Hoffman answered. She called Miranda, who was asleep, to the front door. Cooley and Young asked him to accompany them to the police station to discuss a case that they were investigating. At police headquarters in downtown Phoenix, the detectives placed Miranda in a lineup, and he was identified by Lois Ann Jameson, who remained behind a one-way mirror. She wasn't certain that she could identify her abductor but thought that Miranda was the most similar. She asked whether she could hear him speak.

The detectives went back to Miranda, told him that he had been identified, and began questioning him in greater detail. This took place in the station house interrogation room, which was off-limits to everyone except the police and suspects. The two detectives testified at Miranda's trial that "neither threats nor promises had been made." They simply questioned Miranda, who admitted that he had raped Jameson and confessed to a second robbery that had occurred on November 27, 1962. Miranda's memory of the interrogation was not quite so bland. He recalled:

A police photo shows Twila Hoffman's 1953 Packard parked outside the Mesa, Arizona, house that she shared with Ernest Miranda.

Once they get you in a little room and they start badgering you one way or the other, "you better tell us . . . or we're going to throw the book at you" . . . that is what was told to me. They would throw the book at me. They would try to give me all the time they could. They thought there was even the possibility that there was something wrong with me. They would try to help me, get me medical care if I needed it. . . . And I haven't had any sleep since the day before. I'm tired. I just got off work, and they have me and they are interrogating me. They mention first one crime, then another one, they are certain I am the person . . . knowing what a penitentiary is like, a person has to be frightened, scared. And not knowing if he'll be able to get back up and go home.[1]

The detectives next brought Jameson into the interrogation room so she could hear Miranda's voice. They turned to him and asked whether she was the victim, and he answered affirmatively, believing that Jameson had already identified him in the lineup. The police then typed out Miranda's statement confessing to the crime, noting that Miranda was confessing voluntarily. The following is the essence of Miranda's confession in his own, halting words:

Seen a girl walking up street stopped a little ahead of her got out of car walked towards her grabbed her by the arm and asked to get into the car. Got in car without force tied hands & ankles. Drove away for a few miles. Stopped asked to take clothes off. Did not, asked me to take her back home. I started to take clothes off her without any force. And

*with cooperation. Asked her to lay down and
she did, could not get penis into vagina got
about ¹⁄₂ (half) inch in. Told her to get clothes
back on. Drove her home. I couldn't say I was
sorry for what I had done. But asked her to
say a prayer for me.*[2]

By 1:30 P.M., after only two hours, the entire interrogation and confession were completed. No evidence of police brutality. Nothing apparently out of the ordinary. Yet within three years these few hours in the lives of Ernest Miranda and Detectives Cooley and Young would create a landmark Supreme Court decision that would send long-lasting reverberations throughout the entire U.S. criminal justice system.

Miranda was taken from the interrogation room to the Phoenix city jail, where he was booked on charges of kidnapping and rape. The next day he was taken to the Maricopa County jail. On March 15, he was arraigned on the two charges before a justice of the peace. In addition, he was charged with the other robbery that he had confessed committing; Miranda always maintained that the police had promised he would not be prosecuted for this crime in exchange for the confession in the Jameson attack.

THE DEFENDANT

Ernest Miranda had led a troubled life prior to his encounter with the Phoenix police in March 1963. He was born in Mesa, Arizona, in 1940. His father, Manuel, had come to Arizona from Sonora, Mexico, and had tried to earn a living as a house painter. When Ernest was six years old, his mother died. His father remarried the following year. His mother's death seemed to mark the end of a happy childhood and the beginning of a troubled youth. Ernest never got along with his stepmother and soon drifted apart from his father. He never developed close relationships with any of his four older brothers.

Ernest's difficulties began in elementary school. He was a persistent disciplinary problem, and his attendance record showed more absences than days present. He was able to finish eighth grade in 1954, but Ernest's final year of education was blemished by his arrest for car theft—the first time he was charged with a serious crime. He was convicted and received a probationary sentence, which seemed to have little impact on his antisocial behavior because he was arrested less than a year later for burglary. Following this conviction, he was sent to the Arizona State Industrial School for Boys at Fort Grant. This brief exposure to the penal system also had no apparent effect on Ernest. Only a month after his release from Fort Grant in January 1956, he was arrested again, this time for an even more serious charge of attempted rape and assault. He was found guilty and returned to Fort Grant to serve a one-year sentence.

In January 1957, the sixteen-year-old was released again from Fort Grant and decided to leave Arizona and start anew in California. Unfortunately his problems with the law followed him, and in May he was arrested for curfew violations and Peeping Tom activities, which earned him a three-day stay in the Los Angeles County House of Detention. Afterwards, Ernest was able to stay out of trouble for nearly five months, working as a delivery boy for a grocery store. In September, however, he was again arrested. This time the charge was a serious one: armed robbery. Although the state did not have enough evidence to convict, state officials were tired of his presence in its juvenile courts, and a judge ordered him sent back to Arizona.

Miranda (number 1) appears in a Phoenix Police Department lineup. After Lois Ann Jameson tentatively picked him out as her attacker, two Phoenix detectives obtained a confession from Miranda in which he admitted kidnapping and raping Jameson.

In the four years prior to his eighteenth birthday, Ernest Miranda had accumulated a record of six arrests and four convictions. He decided that it was time to attempt a new start in his life; he believed that the military would provide a new opportunity to become a productive citizen. Unfortunately, Miranda's problems were not restricted to the civilian world, and within a very short time he was in trouble again, spending six of his fifteen months in the U.S. Army at hard labor in the post stockade at Fort Campbell in Kentucky. In July 1959, he received an undesirable discharge. The army, like the California juvenile court, made Miranda visit a psychiatrist, but both times the efforts were short-lived and had little effect.

Miranda spent the next several months wandering somewhat aimlessly through the South, until he was arrested in December 1959 in Nashville, Tennessee, for driving a stolen car. He pleaded guilty to the charges and was sentenced to a year in federal prison in Ohio. After two months, Miranda requested a transfer to a federal facility closer to his family in Arizona. His request was granted, and he served the remaining portion of his sentence in Lompoc, California, until his release in January 1961.

Following his release from federal prison, the next two years of Miranda's life assumed a calm and near-normal state. He met Twila Hoffman, who was eight years older than him and separated from her husband. He soon moved in with Hoffman and her ten-year-old daughter and eleven-year-old son. Miranda and his new family returned to Mesa, Arizona, where Twila was able to find a job at a local nursery school. Ernest, however, was forced to take a series of short-term, poor-paying menial jobs. Finally in August 1962 he landed a job loading trucks at

United Produce in Phoenix. It seemed for a while that Miranda's life had taken a turn for the better. Unfortunately this illusion was shattered less than eight months later when he was roused from his sleep on March 13, 1963, by two Phoenix detectives.

THE TRIAL

Because Miranda was indigent, or poor, the Maricopa County Court appointed an attorney to assist him at his trial, which was scheduled for May 14, 1963. His attorney would be Alvin Moore, an elderly lawyer who had built up a successful civil practice after moving to Phoenix in 1951. Moore would receive one hundred dollars from Maricopa County for defending Miranda at his trial and another one hundred dollars if he chose to appeal. Although neither very experienced in criminal law nor particularly attracted to its challenges, Moore believed that he had a civic duty to volunteer as a court-appointed lawyer for poor defendants. Having heard of a recent shortage, he had added his name to the county's list of available attorneys a few months before Miranda's arrest.

Moore had represented criminal defendants before coming to Arizona, but he was somewhat rusty in the practice of criminal law. His initial strategy in Miranda's case was to pursue an insanity defense. On May 14, the trial court appointed two psychiatrists to examine Miranda, and a new trial date was set the following month. Dr. Lee Rubinow examined Miranda twice and declared him to be "oriented in all spheres" but "immature; psychologically and somewhat inadequate. . . . There is, emotionality, instability and inability to control."[3] Unfortunately for Moore and his client, Rubinow went on to note that in his opinion Miranda "is not insane nor mentally defective, he knows the difference between right and wrong, he knows the consequences of his acts."[4] A second psychiatrist, Dr. James Kilgore, examined Miranda and reached an almost identical conclusion. The court directed the defense and prosecution to prepare for the trial scheduled on June 20, 1963.

Miranda's trial was perfunctory, completely lacking in anything dramatic. Neither the prosecution nor defense made an effort at flowery oratory; no legal surprises or last-minute witnesses livened up the proceedings. The only emotional moment came during Lois Ann Jameson's testimony as she quietly recounted her ordeal. Deputy County Attorney Lawrence Turoff called four witnesses to prove his case—Jameson, her sister, and Detectives Cooley and Young—and presented Miranda's written confession. The defense did little more than challenge the use of the confession. Moore offered no evidence and called no witnesses, although he did engage in a somewhat spirited cross-examination of Jameson, pointing out the inconsistencies in her testimony and trying to undermine her credibility. Bothered by how the police had extracted the confession from his client, Moore questioned Detective Cooley thoroughly during cross-examination. The attorney hoped to appeal to sympathetic members of the jury by demonstrating coercion and station house intimidation, but he did not feel confident about his chances for success.

After both sides had presented their case, Judge Yale McFate, a six-year veteran of the Maricopa County Superior Court, gave his instructions to the jury in a straight-forward and easily understandable manner. He very carefully explained Arizona's law on the use of confessions and reminded the jury that he had allowed Miranda's confession to be admitted into evidence over the objections of the defense counsel. The judge noted that the jury need not be limited by his ruling and should determine for themselves whether the confession had been obtained voluntarily. He provided the legal definitions of the terms *coercion* and *voluntariness* and discussed the problems caused by police violence, threats, or promises of immunity, all of which could render a confession involuntary and, therefore, inadmissible. McFate's final instruction on confessions, the instruction that would eventually become a major constitutional issue, was: "The fact that a defendant was under arrest at the time he made a confession or that he was not at the time represented by counsel or that he was not told that any statement he might make could or would be used against him, in and of themselves, will not render such a confession involuntary."[5]

The jury of nine men and three women then retired to deliberate the case. Five hours later they returned with a verdict of guilty to both the kidnapping and raping of Lois Ann Jameson. On June 27, 1963, Miranda returned to court for his sentence. Judge McFate sentenced him to serve two concurrent terms (running simultaneously rather than one after the other), twenty to thirty years on each charge, at the Arizona State Prison at Florence.

Chapter 2

REACHING THE SUPREME COURT

With his client incarcerated in the state prison at Florence, Alvin Moore reviewed the way that the Phoenix police had interrogated Ernest Miranda and the manner in which he had been convicted at his trial. Moore was convinced that Miranda had not received a fair trial and that the most incriminating piece of evidence, his confession, should not have been admitted as evidence. He realized that he did not have a very strong case, particularly in light of existing state law, but he felt compelled to challenge Miranda's conviction and appeal to the Arizona Supreme Court.

APPEALING TO THE ARIZONA SUPREME COURT

Moore filed his brief with the Arizona Supreme Court on December 10, 1963, approximately five months after Miranda had been sentenced. (A brief is a document in which an attorney presents his or her legal arguments on behalf of a client.) Moore's brief dealt almost entirely with the issue of whether Miranda's confession had been made voluntarily. He argued that the confession had been made involuntarily and that Miranda had never been warned when he made his oral confession that these statements could be used against him. Additionally, the written statements he signed never specified which rights he was supposed to have been made aware of by his interrogators. Moore also emphasized the intimidating effect the station house and the unfriendly confines of the interrogation room had upon his client, a young Mexican-American of limited education. Although Moore realized that his brief found little support from Arizona precedents (earlier court decisions), he nevertheless believed that the U.S. Constitution and the Bill of Rights provided guarantees that were denied to his client. (The Bill of Rights, contained in the first ten amendments to the U.S. Constitution, declare the basic rights and protections from the federal government.)

Miranda and his attorney waited for more than a year before they heard a response from the Arizona Supreme Court. The five justices handed down their decision on April 22, 1965. Justice Ernest W. McFarland, a former Arizona governor and U.S. senator, delivered the opinion. Despite being the newest member of the court, having only joined it two months earlier, McFarland had been assigned to write what most members of Arizona's highest court believed to be a very important case. In the preceding year, the U.S. Supreme Court had decided in *Escobedo v. Illinois* (1964) that defendants had a right to an attorney, if they requested one, as soon as they were taken into custody and that the police must effectively warn suspects of their constitutional right to remain silent. The *Escobedo* case sent shock waves around the nation, alerting police and prosecutors that they may soon be facing tighter restrictions on their procedures when they had suspects in their custody, especially in regard to the presence of defense attorneys and the constitutionality of confessions.

Criminal justice officials in Arizona were greatly relieved when Justice McFarland delivered his opinion for the unanimous court in the *Miranda* case. The first thing Justice McFarland did was to attempt to distinguish *Miranda* from the *Escobedo* decision. McFarland listed the following circumstances, which he believed the U.S. Supreme Court required in *Escobedo v. Illinois* before determining that a defendant's constitutional rights had been denied:

1. The general inquiry by police into an unsolved crime must have begun to focus on a particular suspect.
2. The suspect must have been taken into police custody.
3. The police in its interrogation must have elicited an incriminating statement.
4. The suspect must have requested and been denied an opportunity to consult with his lawyer.
5. The police must not have effectively warned the suspect of his constitutional right to remain silent.[1]

McFarland reasoned that although the facts of Miranda's case had satisfied the first three criteria, it differed from *Escobedo* on the final two. Miranda apparently had not requested an attorney during the custodial stage (during interrogation) and, therefore, had not been positively refused one. On the final point of whether Miranda had been warned of his constitutional right to remain silent, the facts were in dispute. McFarland, however, resolved the issue by reasoning that the "defendant had a record which indicated that he was not without court-room experience . . . he was certainly not unfamiliar with legal proceedings and his rights in court. The police testified they had informed the defendant of his rights, and he had stated in his written confession that he understood his rights, which would certainly include the right to counsel, and it is not for this court to dispute his statement that he did. His experience under previous cases would indicate that his statement that he understood his rights was true."[2]

Justice McFarland ended his opinion by clarifying the central issue in the appeal: whether Miranda's confession had been voluntary. The court concluded that Detectives Cooley and Young had not coerced the defendant's statement. No threats or promises had been made, and despite his limited education Miranda had understood his rights. On these grounds, the Arizona Supreme Court confirmed his conviction.

AN APPEAL TO THE FEDERAL COURTS

Following his unsuccessful appeal to the Arizona Supreme Court, Ernest Miranda decided to turn to the federal courts and seek a reversal of his conviction by appealing to the U.S. Supreme Court. He had now been in prison for two years and was anxious to have what he believed to be a more sympathetic court review his case. Miranda, like many other impoverished state prisoners who wished to appeal their cases, had heard about the good fortune of Clarence Gideon, who had appealed his conviction *in*

CURRENT ARREST OR RECEIPT

DATE ARRESTED OR RECEIVED	CHARGE OR OFFENSE (If code citation is used it should be accompanied by charge)	DISPOSITION OR SENTENCE (List FINAL disposition only. If not now available, submit later on FBI Form R–84 for completion of record.)
-5-1963 ARICOPA COUNTY	COUNT I-KIDNAPPING COUNT II-RAPE(FIRST DEGREE) TO RUN CONCURRENTLY	20 yrs.to 30 yrs.

OCCUPATION	RESIDENCE OF PERSON FINGERPRINTED
TRUCK DRIVER	WIFE: TWILA MIRANDA 157 E. COMMONWELL CHANDLER, ARIZONA

If COLLECT wire reply or COLLECT telephone reply is desired, indicate here

☐ Wire reply   ☐ Telephone reply

Telephone number

FOR INSTITUTIONS USE ONLY

Sentence expires... 7-5-1993 ....

INSTRUCTIONS

1. FORWARD ARREST CARDS TO FBI IMMEDIATELY AFTER FINGERPRINTING FOR MOST EFFECTIVE SERVICE.
2. TYPE or PRINT all information.
3. Note amputations in proper finger squares.
4. REPLY WILL QUOTE ONLY NUMBER APPEARING IN THE BLOCK MARKED "CONTRIBUTOR'S NO."
5. Indicate any additional copies for other agencies in space below—include their complete mailing address.

SEND COPY TO:

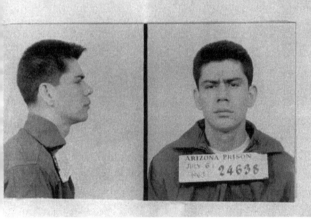

Joe M. Rodriguez, Secretary
ARIZONA STATE PRISON
Florence, Arizona

This arrest card details the facts of Miranda's conviction. A jury convicted Miranda of kidnapping and first-degree rape, and Judge Yale McFate gave Miranda a sentence of twenty to thirty years.

forma pauperis (a Latin phrase meaning "in the form of a pauper").

Gideon had been arrested for breaking into a Panama City, Florida, poolroom. Unable to afford a lawyer, he had asked the trial court to provide an attorney to defend him, but the court had refused his request. Gideon was found guilty and sentenced to five years in prison. With the assistance of an eminent lawyer, Abe Fortas, he was able to have his conviction overturned in 1963 by the U.S. Supreme Court, which ruled that poor defendants had a constitutional right to legal representation at their trial. Gideon was tried again for the break-in, this time with a lawyer, and he was acquitted.

Miranda likewise filed an appeal *in forma pauperis* to the U.S. Supreme Court in late spring 1965. His petition was returned in June, however, because he had failed to include an affidavit confirming his inability to pay and a copy of the final judgment against him by the Arizona Supreme Court. Unknown to Miranda, however, his case had captured the attention of the Phoenix office of the American Civil Liberties Union (ACLU). For the past half century, this organization had provided legal assistance through a nationwide network of volunteer lawyers for indigent defendants whose constitutional rights were believed to have been violated. Robert Corcoran, a volunteer who headed the Phoenix ACLU office, helped provide lawyers for poor defendants in Arizona. Corcoran had taken notice of the Arizona Supreme Court's decision in Miranda's appeal. Having worked briefly as a local prosecutor, he was familiar with the Arizona law pertaining to the taking of confessions and with police custodial practices. He thought Miranda's case presented interesting issues at a time when they were ripe for consideration by the federal courts, especially by the U.S. Supreme Court.

Corcoran immediately wrote a letter to Miranda's original lawyer, Alvin Moore, informing Moore of his interest in the case and its potential for success at the federal level. Corcoran told Moore that the ACLU would help him prepare the case for the Supreme Court and offer whatever assistance it could. Moore declined Corcoran's offer. He said he lacked the necessary funds and the physical endurance to pursue the Miranda case any further. Corcoran quickly sought to find another lawyer whom he felt would be as excited about Miranda's case as he was. He had recently met a young Phoenix attorney, Rex E. Lee, who had just moved from Washington, D.C., where he had worked as a law clerk for Supreme Court justice Byron White. Corcoran was impressed by Lee's knowledge of federal court procedures and concluded that the young attorney was the ideal candidate to handle the Miranda appeal. Corcoran was disappointed when Lee notified him of a Supreme Court rule that prohibited its former clerks from representing clients before the Court for a period of two years.

Undaunted by the lack of success with his first two choices, Corcoran next contacted John J. Flynn, an experienced trial attorney with Lewis and Roca, one of Phoenix's most prestigious law firms. The firm prided itself on community service and pro bono legal assistance. (Pro bono—from the Latin phrase *pro bono publico,* "for the public good"— refers to legal work that is donated free of charge.) A specialist in criminal law, Flynn was genuinely excited by the prospects of Miranda's case and turned to his associate, John Paul Frank, for assistance. Frank was a nationally renowned authority on the

Bill of Rights and well versed with the procedures of the federal appeals courts. Not only did both men jump at the chance to become involved in what they sensed was a very important case, they told Corcoran that their law firm would bear the costs. Corcoran then notified Miranda of his good fortune in having two superb attorneys take his case into the federal appeals process. An elated Ernest Miranda wrote back to Corcoran from his prison cell: "Your letter . . . has made me very happy. To know that someone has taken an interest in my case, has increased my moral (sic) enormously. . . . I would appreciate if you or either Mr. Flynn keep me informed of any and all results. I also want to thank you and Mr. Flynn for all you are doing for me."[3]

Miranda's two lawyers were an interesting pair whose professional and personality differences seemed to complement each other. John Flynn was an energized, dramatic champion of the underdog. After graduating from the University of Arizona Law School with only average grades, he struck out on his own, taking any case that would help pay the rent. He soon developed a reputation as a spirited and effective litigator, which led to a two-year stint in the county prosecutor's office. Even after joining the prestigious Lewis and Roca law firm and becoming its chief trial attorney, he continued to maintain his image as a totally dedicated, pugnacious advocate. He made no moral judgments about his clients. His loyalty was to the law, and he worked selflessly. Flynn once described the demands of his criminal practice: "It gets to you . . . the most difficult case . . . is the case in which you're satisfied your client is innocent and indeed he is innocent. That's the case that really burns you up. Emotionally and otherwise . . . because there's the potential through your fault of an innocent man being convicted because you did not do something, or you did something you should not have done. You have to live with it."[4]

Miranda's other lawyer, John Paul Frank, had followed a very different route to the Lewis and Roca law firm. A Wisconsin native, Frank had earned B.A., M.A., and LL.B. (Bachelor of Laws) degrees from the University of Wisconsin before going on to earn a J.S.D. (Doctor of Science of Law degree) from Yale Law School. He had clerked for Supreme Court justice Hugo Black in 1942 and taught American legal history at several prestigious universities, including Indiana and Yale. He was the author of several books on the history of the Supreme Court, including a recent constitutional law casebook. Frank was not merely a typical academic theoretician or armchair speculator who spouted his opinions about the U.S. legal system. He had been involved in several civil rights cases, frequently authoring amicus curiae (a Latin phrase meaning "friend of the court") briefs supporting the NAACP and its chief litigator at the time, Thurgood Marshall. By 1965 Frank had become a respected member of the firm, specializing in appellate work. His style was urbane and intellectual, yet he, like Flynn, was dogged in his commitment to progressive principles of law and the rights of clients. Both men were determined to get the U.S. Supreme Court to review Ernest Miranda's case.

GAINING THE ATTENTION OF THE SUPREME COURT

The Supreme Court is besieged by many more appeals than it can possibly decide. In 1925 Congress eased the Court's steadily increasing caseload by giving it more discretion in selecting which cases it wanted to review. Instead of legislating mandatory appeals, this act provided that appellants could request that the Supreme Court hear their cases by filing petitions for certiorari. (Certiorari is a formal order, or writ, issued by the U.S. Supreme Court to a lower court that requires the transfer of the lower court's records and proceedings in a particular case to the Supreme Court for review.) The justices then developed their own informal procedure, known as the rule of four, to help them implement their new power of case selection. The justices of the Supreme Court meet in a secret conference, and for a case to be selected for review at least four members must agree that an appeal deserves to be granted full consideration by the entire Court because it presents an important issue of federal or constitutional law. If four justices vote to grant certiorari, a date for the appeal's oral arguments is scheduled.

By the mid-1960s, when Ernest Miranda appealed his case to the Supreme Court, the Court was receiving more than two thousand appeals each year. It could only decide between 150 and 175 cases a year, thus making the odds about ten-to-one against Miranda being granted his petition. (By the mid-1990s, the number of appeals had climbed to more than five thousand cases, lowering each appellant's odds to less than one chance in twenty-five.)[5]

Rule 22 (1) of the Supreme Court procedures required a writ of certiorari to be filed within ninety days after the final lower court judgment. Because two months had already elapsed since the decision of the Arizona Supreme Court, Flynn and Frank had just a month to convince the U.S. Supreme Court that Ernest Miranda's case deserved to be placed on the Court's 1965–66 docket. By the beginning of the fall term more than one hundred cases involving issues related to its *Escobedo* decision had reached the Supreme Court. The attorneys and defendants in each of these cases hoped to obtain a writ of certiorari and be placed on that year's schedule. For Miranda, his chance came when the Court considered whether to grant him an appeal in their November 22, 1965, conference.

THE COURT

Whenever scholars analyze a significant shift in the direction of Supreme Court policy, they customarily explain such modifications by pointing to changes in the Court's personnel. In attempting to apply this theory to Miranda's case, especially as it was about to be discussed for the first time by the entire Court in its conference, there had been only a single addition to the Court since *Escobedo*. Associate Justice Abe Fortas had just joined the Court in October, replacing Arthur Goldberg, who had resigned in order to replace Adlai Stevenson as the U.S. ambassador to the United Nations. Fortas and Goldberg, however, were ideologically paired on nearly all issues, especially those involving concerns related to due process rights.

The remaining eight members of the Court in fall 1965 had all been on the Court since 1962. After Fortas, the next most junior member of the Court was Byron White, a Kennedy appointment in 1962. Although many viewed White as being liberal because of his aggressive civil rights work while serving in the Justice Department, his position on issues involving the due process rights of defendants was much more conservative and significantly less predictable. He had been a brilliant law student at Yale, an all-American football player at the University of Colorado, as well as a wartime friend of President John F. Kennedy.

The oldest members of the Court, Hugo Black and William Douglas, were President Franklin D. Roosevelt appointees with strong reputations as civil

The justices of the U.S. Supreme Court pose for this 1965 portrait. Sitting (left to right) Tom Clark, Hugo Black, Chief Justice Earl Warren, William Douglas, and John Harlan; standing (left to right) Byron White, William Brennan, Potter Stewart, and Abe Fortas.

libertarians. Douglas, especially, was in the forefront of the chief justice's due process revolution and could be counted upon to use the *Miranda* case as a mechanism for expanding the rights of defendants.

Although appointed to the Court by President Dwight D. Eisenhower, a Republican, William Brennan was a lifelong Democrat whose father had been an active union leader in Hudson County, New Jersey. Brennan would continue to fight for civil liberties issues into the 1990s as a member of the Burger and Rehnquist Courts. He would often be a lonely liberal voice in his twilight years on the bench, but in the mid-1960s he joined with Warren, Black, Douglas, and Fortas to form the heart of the Court's seemingly prodefendant posture.

Chief Justice Earl Warren, the leader and namesake of this Court, was a former California governor and longtime influential figure in the Republican party. He began his political career in Oakland as Alameda County prosecutor, but by the time he reached the Supreme Court his views had moved so far to the left that Eisenhower would later lament that Warren's appointment was his greatest mistake as president.

The remaining trio of justices, John Marshall Harlan, Tom C. Clark, and Potter Stewart, were most likely to reject Miranda's appeal and find the Phoenix police procedures acceptable and the resulting confession admissible. Harlan was the grandson and namesake of the great dissenter of the Waite, Fuller, and White Courts. The elder Harlan's most famous dissent came in *Plessy v. Ferguson* (1896), a case that was eventually overruled by *Brown v. Board of Education of Topeka* (1954*)*, a decision in which the younger Harlan joined a unanimous majority opinion that cited his grandfather's prophetic dissent. Harlan had been named to the Supreme Court by Eisenhower in 1954, following the death of Justice Robert H. Jackson. Prior to the appointment he had been an assistant U.S. attorney and a member of a prestigious Wall Street law firm. Shortly after becoming president, Eisenhower had named Harlan to the Federal Circuit Court of Appeals in New York, where he sat for only a year before reaching the Supreme Court.

Justice Clark, President Harry S. Truman's third appointment to the Supreme Court, was a well-known Texas politician. Clark had risen in governmental service under the tutelage of powerful Texas senator Tom Connally. Clark served in various important positions within the U.S. Justice Department, including being head of both the antitrust and criminal divisions. He also oversaw the relocation of Japanese-Americans banished from the West Coast during World War II. In 1945, Truman named Clark as U.S. attorney general, the head of the entire Justice Department. In 1949, following the death of Justice Frank Murphy, Truman appointed Clark to the highest court. Given Clark's long service as a federal prosecutor, Court observers expected that he would not be very sympathetic to Ernest Miranda's appeal.

The final member of the trio, Justice Stewart, was appointed to the Court by Eisenhower in 1958 to replace the retiring Justice Harold Burton. Stewart was part of a well-connected Ohio family, closely associated with powerful Republican senator Robert Taft. Stewart attended law school at Yale University and returned to Cincinnati after graduation to practice law. In 1954, Eisenhower named him to the Federal Circuit Court of Appeals for the Sixth District, where he served for four years. Ideologically, Justice Stewart was typically described as a centrist on the Warren Court, but like Clark, Harlan, and White, he had definite prosecutorial leanings.

During its conference of November 22, 1965, the Court granted certiorari in the case of *Miranda v. Arizona*. For the Court, the somewhat enigmatic *Escobedo* decision had raised more questions than it answered, and now it was time for it to confront and resolve these issues, which were most basic to a defendant's due process guarantees. In his insightful analysis of what has been called the due process revolution, Fred Graham has noted:

The Arizona State Prison is located in Florence. Ernest Miranda had been assigned to the Florence facility following his conviction, and he remained incarcerated there while his case was on appeal to the U.S. Supreme Court.

The Court had turned a corner in Escobedo, *but the opinion did not say where the new course would lead. It said only that when the criminal justice process shifts from investigatory to accusatory . . . our adversary system begins to operate, and under the circumstances, the accused must be permitted to consult with his lawyer. . . . If a person had a constitutional right to his lawyer's counsel during interrogation, then didn't he have to be informed of that fact before any question-*

ing? If he asked to see his lawyer, didn't all questioning have to cease until the lawyer arrived? If he wanted a lawyer but could not afford one, didn't the state have to provide counsel?[6]

John Flynn and John Paul Frank rejoiced when they heard that the Supreme Court had agreed to rule on Ernest Miranda's case. They immediately set about building the strongest possible case by reviewing legal precedents, shaping their arguments, and plotting their strategies.

Chapter 3

THE CONSTITUTIONAL BACKGROUND

Professor Frances Allen, the former dean of the University of Michigan Law School, has written that a "great" Supreme Court decision is one that "appears to capture the essence of an era, because it epitomizes the tensions and social pathology of the period, and at the same time, casts revealing light on its ideals and aspirations."[1] The *Miranda* case clearly satisfies Professor Allen's definition of greatness, and it has been characterized as a decision that symbolized the entire due process revolution.

The due process revolution refers to a series of constitutional law decisions handed down by Chief Justice Earl Warren and his colleagues on the bench during the 1960s and included such procedural issues as a defendant's right to an attorney, the right to exclude evidence seized illegally by the police, the right to a jury trial, and the protection against coerced confessions. Law professor Craig Bradley summarizes this development by writing that this revolution in criminal procedure extends to the "entire range of activities associated with bringing a defendant to trial. It begins with investigation by the police, including searches of houses, cars, and so on, and lineups and photo displays of potential suspects; it proceeds through arrest, interrogation, arraignment, preliminary hearing, indictment by grand jury, trial, sentencing, appeal, and collateral challenges to conviction."[2]

Despite the close association in the public's mind between the *Miranda* case and the issue of coerced confessions, the case also involved critical right-to-counsel issues, as well as a series of even broader constitutional questions related to federalism and the due process clause of the Fourteenth Amendment. This chapter will discuss all of these basic constitutional questions, the same ones encountered by the *Miranda* lawyers as they prepared their arguments for the Supreme Court. We will begin with a close look at coerced confessions and the Fifth Amendment.

CONFESSIONS AND THE FIFTH AMENDMENT

Like so many of the protections offered by the federal Bill of Rights to persons accused of crimes, the Fifth Amendment protection against forced self-incrimination reflects the competing interests of society versus the rights of the individual. Citizens have the expectation that government will protect them from criminals and will attempt to ensure that their community and property will be safe and secure. On the other hand, the U.S. Constitution guarantees that once a person is accused of a crime, he or she will be treated fairly and receive due process of law. A suspect's right to be protected from physical and psychological coercion by police officials in their efforts to extract a confession is one of the most basic guarantees set forth in the Bill of Rights.

There are many reasons why it is so important to have the Fifth Amendment's protection against coerced confessions. The first, and possibly most obvious, objection to a coerced confession is its questionable reliability. What good is a confession that has been beaten out of an individual or obtained as the result of threats or torture? The accused is simply attempting to stop the pain or prevent future pain. A person in this situation may say anything, simply telling his or her accusers whatever they wish to hear. The reliability of such statements obtained under physical or emotional duress is clearly suspect.

A second reason relates to the very essence of the U.S. justice system. Because we have an adversarial system in which the prosecutor has the burden of proof in criminal cases to establish guilt beyond a reasonable doubt, defendants have the right to remain silent throughout the entire proceedings from arrest through trial. The accused is not compelled to assist the prosecution in any way and is constitutionally guaranteed the right to silence through the Fifth Amendment. This protection against self-incrimination is also consistent with our constitutional guarantee of a fair trial in which due process of law must be satisfied before an individual can be punished—that is, lose his or her life, liberty, or property. The police and prosecution, therefore, must be able to prove their case without necessarily forcing the accused to cooperate or assist them in their efforts to ascertain guilt. This is the way our justice system has been formulated since its inception in the late eighteenth century.

Although it is commonly assumed that the first instances of coerced confessions and their eventual resolution had their roots in medieval England, historians have traced instances of the problem all the way back to early Egyptian times, where the first illustrations of police were found on tombs dated about 2000 B.C. The police were depicted beating a suspect.[3] Famous historical figures—including Joan of Arc, Savonarola, and Galileo—were also victims of coercive questioning, especially during the Inquisition. (The Inquisition was a court of the Roman Catholic Church that tried persons accused of heresy, or having opinions that conflicted with Church doctrine.) In their recent book on confessions, legal historians Lawrence S. Wrightsman and Saul M. Kassin describe these historical incidents:

Joan was subjected to prolonged and relentless questioning, accompanied by the threat of torture. . . . Savonarola was a priest in Florence who denounced the immoralities of the Papacy. After being tortured in 1498, he agreed to make any confession his inquisitors wished from him. Galileo was torn between his allegiance to the Church and his observations of the solar system as a scientist. Broken and ill at the age of 70, and having been shown the instruments of torture, he recanted his advocacy of the sun as the center of our planetary system.

The Salem witch trials, in Massachusetts in 1692, were an American manifestation of the use of torture to generate false confessions. Sleep deprivation, forced exercise such as standing for a very long period, and insertion of pins into the bodies of the young women were among the devices to get them to confess to their possession by Satan. Ann Foster, for example, confessed that the devil appeared to her in the shape of a bird on several occasions.[4]

Appearing before officials of the Inquisition, Italian astronomer, physicist, and philosopher Galileo (1564–1642) faces accusations of heresy. The tribunal pressured Galileo to renounce some of his scientific beliefs. Torture, threats, and coercive questioning were among the methods used to obtain confessions and retractions during the Inquisition.

The framers of the Constitution and the Bill of Rights were keenly aware of the English experience with coerced confessions during the sixteenth and seventeenth centuries, when political and religious dissenters were tortured in governmental inquisitions. American legal scholar John H. Wigmore has provided the definitive historical analysis of this period, observing that "up to the middle of the 1600s, at least, the use of torture to extract confessions was common and . . . confessions so obtained were employed evidently without scruple."[5] By the reign (1625–49) of Charles I, the right against self-incrimination began to appear in English common law as a response to the king's increasingly repressive measures, taken against his most persistent critics. Kassin and Wrightsman note that "beginning with the period after the Restoration of 1660, there was a slow and gradual improvement in the procedures used in criminal trials in England. But not until one hundred years later in 1775, in *Rudds Case*, did a judge for the first time place any restrictions on the admissibility of an ordinary confession. And shortly after that, in 1783, the modern view on the admissibility of confessions received what Wigmore called a 'full and clear expression,' that is, that confessions were obtained through promises or threats were not to receive credit as evidence."[6]

Eminent American legal historian Leonard Levy believes that the origins of the right against self-incrimination go back even further. Levy writes: "The story begins even before Magna Carta (1215), because the English legal system—and therefore the American—owes so much to Henry II who ruled England in the last half of the twelfth century. Magna Carta itself first became the talismanic [magical] symbol and source of individual freedom in connection with the struggle against compulsory self-accusation."[7]

Regardless of the exact time when the right against self-incrimination originated in England, historians generally agree that by the second half of the eighteenth century, nearly all of the American colonies had adopted most elements of English common law, including the protection against coerced

A facsimile of the Magna Carta, the 1215 document guaranteeing that the power of the English monarchy would be limited by law. In addition to a provision mandating that the king could not imprison a free man or deprive him of his property except by the judgment of his peers or the law of the land, the Magna Carta provided the basis for the right against self-incrimination in English law.

confessions. Law professor Stephen Markham notes
that as the colonies declared their independence "at
least nine of the new states adopted constitutional
provisions recognizing some type of right against
self-incrimination. Several state ratifying conven-
tions called for the addition of a comparable provision to the federal Constitution. At the Virginia
convention, Patrick Henry spoke specifically of the
need for a measure to prevent the use of torture as a
means of inducing confessions."[8] It was clear from
the discussions at the various state assemblies that
Americans were adamantly opposed to interrogations in which an accused would be tortured until he
or she confessed. The answer was to create procedural guarantees prohibiting such coercive measures.

Following the successful conclusion of the war
against England, the United States had to formulate
its new government. By 1787 the new Constitution
was created, but many people thought there was a
need for a series of amendments that would specify
basic protections to individual Americans from arbi-
trary and oppressive actions by their newly formed
government. Thus in 1789, James Madison introduced a group of proposed amendments to Congress
in response to the public outcry for a bill of individual rights to expand the Constitution, which was in
the process of being ratified. Madison stated that the
protection against self-incrimination should provide
that "no person . . . shall be compelled to be witness
against himself."[9] Madison's proposal was slightly
amended by John Laurence of New York, who limited the self-incrimination provision to only criminal
matters. Professor Markham concluded that when
the proposed Bill of Rights amendments were next
debated in the Senate, the self-incrimination provision was included within the Fifth Amendment,
probably reflecting an attempt "to make it applica-

ble at pretrial stages, a point that would be consistent with the common law scope of the right."[10]

Initially the Fifth Amendment was thought to be a necessary protection against the traditional common-law practice of judicial interrogation. Midway through the nineteenth century, however, with the development of full-time professional police departments in most cities, magistrates began to forgo pretrial interrogations, deferring to the local police and prosecutors who were arresting and questioning defendants. Interrogations moved from the courthouse to the police station. The role of the courts shifted also from active questioner to responsible overseer of police interrogation.

A significant consequence of this shift in interrogation responsibilities was the recurrence of abusive police practices, which were soon characterized in the newspapers as "the third degree." These unlawful police behaviors peaked during the 1920s and 1930s and were documented by the well-publicized Wickersham Commission Report on Law Enforcement (1931). The more blatant abuses by police in coercing confessions through physical means lessened by the 1940s, but police began to use various psychological techniques to extract confessions from reluctant suspects. Even today, police often rely on trickery or deceit in the questioning of suspects. There is even a book written by Fred Inbau and J. Reid, *Criminal Interrogation and Confessions*, that outlines twenty-six specific techniques used to interrogate a suspect. The majority of these techniques involve some form of deception.[11]

By the time the Supreme Court heard the *Miranda* case in 1966, it had been obvious for several decades that there was a problem with police coercing confessions from suspects in violation of their Fifth Amendment protections from self-incrimination. Although suspects were no longer physically co-erced, the problem of an accused individual being tricked into making incriminating statements to the police was a national problem that required the intervention of the Supreme Court.

MIRANDA AND THE RIGHT TO COUNSEL

In addition to issues surrounding confessions in violation of the Fifth Amendment, the *Miranda* case also raised the issue of when the right-to-counsel protections of the Sixth Amendment take effect. In *Gideon v. Wainwright* (1963) the Supreme Court established a defendant's right to counsel in all state criminal cases. This meant that state, local, and federal governments had to provide attorneys for any defendant who could not afford counsel. Despite the general significance of the *Gideon* decision, its impact was somewhat diminished by a pair of court-imposed restrictions: the right to counsel would only apply to serious criminal cases in which the defendant faced the possibility of at least a year in prison, and the right applied to the access to legal counsel during the trial. The second limitation inferred that a defendant may not have the right to an attorney during the investigative and pretrial stages of his or her case.

Both the right to counsel and the protection from self-incrimination are important elements guaranteeing a defendant a fair trial and are, therefore, critical aspects of our nation's adversary system. The adversarial system forms the very basis of the U.S. system of justice. The Constitution reinforces this system in which the defense battles the prosecution. It is believed that by having the two advocates battle before an impartial judge and jury, the facts and the resulting verdict will be fairly determined. If the

Representing Virginia in the first House of Representatives, James Madison served as the primary drafter of the Bill of Rights, the first ten amendments to the U.S. Constitution. The Bill of Rights provides basic freedoms, including the right to due process of law and the right against self-incrimination, that the U.S. government cannot deny to individuals.

two sides are to be on equal footing, they both must have access to an attorney, and as we have just noted, the *Gideon* case requires that an attorney be provided for all defendants, regardless of their financial capability beyond the required standard.

MIRANDA AND THE INCORPORATION DOCTRINE

The complex concept of federalism represents another major constitutional doctrine affecting the resolution of the right-to-counsel and protection-from-self-incrimination issues so central to the *Miranda* case. Federalism is a system of government in which power is "divided by written constitution between a central government and regional or sub-divisional governments. Both governments act directly upon the people through their officials and laws. Both are supreme within their proper sphere of authority. (Both must consent to constitutional change)."[12]

The American federal system involves a division and sharing of power between the national government in Washington, D.C., and the fifty state governments. This means that for any criminal defendant, including Ernest Miranda, it is extremely important whether he or she is being arrested by national police—such as agents of the FBI and the Drug Enforcement Agency—or a state or local law enforcement officer. In the former case, the defendant would be charged with breaking the federal criminal code and would turn to the first ten amendments to the U.S. Constitution in order to learn his or her legal rights. If, however, he or she is charged with violating a state criminal law, which in Miranda's case was the Arizona criminal code, the defendant must now refer to state statutes and constitutional provisions for his or her protection. Although many states have copied the federal Bill of Rights rather closely, there are nevertheless significant differences between the guarantees to defendants in the various state justice systems.

Beginning with the ratification of the Fourteenth Amendment to the Constitution in 1868, defendants in state criminal trials, such as Ernest Miranda, were offered an additional source of legal protections beyond whatever their local state laws provided. The Fourteenth Amendment was initially drafted as a means of ensuring that African-Americans, in particular former slaves in the South, would be afforded protection from state governments that had historically treated them so harshly. Nevertheless, the actual wording of the amendment states its application to *all* U.S. citizens regardless of race or particular state citizenship.

For Miranda and other defendants in state criminal proceedings, the relevant clause of the Fourteenth Amendment is found in section one: "nor shall any State deprive any person of life, liberty, or property, without due process of law." What does this rather ambiguous provision mean in terms of Ernest Miranda and his confession? Did his interrogation in a Phoenix police station for two hours without an attorney violate the meaning of this due process clause?

In the 128 years since the ratification of the Fourteenth Amendment, the U.S. Supreme Court has attempted to define the due process clause and determine which procedures and guarantees must be provided by the state courts in order to satisfy the federal due process requirements. The Court has looked to the various provisions of the Bill of Rights as a source of the type of protections necessary to satisfy the due process requirement raised by the Fourteenth Amendment. Although there has never been a willingness to incorporate, or apply, the entire list of Bill of Rights guarantees to state court proceedings, the Supreme Court has selectively chosen certain guarantees listed in the first ten amendments that comprise a type of honor roll of protections against state incursion. Over the years, the Supreme Court has incorporated nearly all of the Bill of Rights guarantees, with the exception of the Fifth Amendment's requirement of indictment by grand jury and the Eighth Amendment's prohibition against excessive bail, into the Fourteenth Amendment.

The Supreme Court began its efforts to define the Fourteenth Amendment's due process clause in the case of *Hurtado v. California* (1884). Writing for the majority, Justice Stanley Matthews explained that due process of law was not to be measured exclusively by the first ten amendments but rather to be defined in terms of the "natural law concepts and the common law experience of the members of the Supreme Court."[13] The Court then moved on a case-by-case basis, deciding which specific rights were sufficiently important to be included within the working definition of the Fourteenth Amendment's due process requirements. Justice Benjamin Cardozo offered one of the best efforts at defining the vague concept of due process in *Palko v. Connecticut* (1937). He wrote that for a guarantee from the Bill of Rights to be made applicable to state action through the Fourteenth Amendment it would have "to be of the very essence of a scheme of ordered liberty and to abolish them would violate a principle of justice so rooted in the traditions of and conscience of our people as to be ranked as fundamental."[14]

The Supreme Court clarified its position on due process and the issue of federalism in *Twining v. New Jersey* (1907). In his majority opinion, Justice William Moody explained:

> *The genius of federalism does not require that the states be permitted to experiment with the*

fundamental rights of defendants. . . . The mere status of being in America should confer protection broad enough to protect any man from the vagaries of a state which by inertia or design fails to keep pace with a national consensus concerning the fundamental rights of the individual in our society."[15]

What did all of this constitutional history and semantic fine-tuning mean for Ernest Miranda and the state of Arizona? By the time the Supreme Court was considering *Miranda*, it had already decided in *Gideon v. Wainwright* (1963) that state criminal defendants had the right to counsel during their trial. It was unclear, however, whether this right would extend to the pretrial period and, in particular, reach the interrogation process following arrest.

With respect to the issue of the Fifth Amendment's guarantee against self-incrimination, the Supreme Court ruled in *Molloy v. Hogan* (1964) that the Fourteenth Amendment's due process clause guaranteed a defendant the protection of the Fifth Amendment's privilege against self-incrimination. Despite the *Molloy* ruling, Miranda wondered whether his interrogation, which lasted several hours and ultimately resulted in his confession to the kidnapping and rape charges, violated the Court's new due process interpretations. He and his attorneys argued that because he was not advised of his right to remain silent and to consult with an attorney, his due process rights had been violated by the state of Arizona.

The membership of the Court during the 1960s was led by Chief Justice Earl Warren, but individual justices, such as Hugo Black, William Douglas, Arthur Goldberg, William Brennan, Thurgood Marshall, and Abe Fortas, provided a consistent bloc of votes ensuring that the Fourteenth Amendment's due process clause would be applied whenever a state failed to guarantee a fundamental right. Although the activist inclinations of the Warren Court were never approximated and were even rejected by several subsequent members of the Supreme Court during the 1970s and 1980s, the Burger and Rehnquist Courts have never directly overruled any of the Warren Court decisions that nationalized so many provisions of the Bill of Rights. The Court has now incorporated nearly every protection offered defendants accused of crimes in state proceedings with the exception of the right to a grand jury indictment. Several decisions have seriously undermined the viability of some of these guarantees, especially in the area of the Fourth Amendment's search-and-seizure restrictions, but the overall commitment of the Supreme Court to protect individual defendants from unconstitutional state procedures has not been abandoned.

CONFESSIONS AND THE POWER OF THE JUDICIARY

The problems of police brutality and coerced confessions have existed within the U.S. criminal justice system for many decades. In his *Crime and Punishment in American History*, Professor Laurence Friedman writes that "police brutality has a long, dishonorable history, not only on the street, but also in the station house. Here was the domain of the third degree—various ways of getting information out of suspects by inflicting suffering, physical or mental. This rather bland phrase conceals a whole world of torture and abuse—beatings with nightsticks and rubber hoses, and sometimes worse. . . . Commission followed commission, investigation followed investigation but brutality always managed to survive."[16] Although the incidence and viciousness of police brutality and coerced confessions had decreased substantially by the time of Ernest Miranda's arrest, the underlying problem of police misconduct still plagued the nation.

Whenever society is faced with a problem, such as controlling police behavior, it has three basic options, each requiring action from one of the three institutions of government: the executive, legislative, or judicial. Because the police themselves are part of the executive branch, albeit at the local level of government, it is logical to expect that police chiefs, prosecutors (district attorneys), or mayors would address the problem and hopefully correct it. If the problem persists, as Professor Friedman has argued, it may then be time to turn the problem over to the legislative branch of government, either a local city council or a statewide (elected) assembly that would enact appropriate legislation. The judiciary, as the third branch, is typically dependent upon the other two branches: the legislative branch for passing the laws and the executive branch for enforcing or implementing the laws. The courts may interpret these laws and declare them constitutional or judge the actions of members of the executive branch, including the police, as they attempt to carry out these laws and prescribed legal responsibilities.

What happens, however, when society is faced with a persistent problem like police brutality, which the branches of government have been either unwilling or unable to resolve? The typical response of the judiciary to this dilemma is to simply do nothing. Because of its restricted power and institutional limitations, the judicial branch has been accurately described by the late Yale law professor Alexander Bickel in the title of his book *The Least Dangerous Branch*. Bickel and others point to the inability of the judiciary to initiate cases involving legal issues that it wishes to decide and to its inability to guarantee compliance with the legal decisions it does make. Because courts must wait for cases to reach their narrowly defined jurisdiction, they are usually incapable of setting an agenda for particular policy issues they may wish to resolve. Additionally, the judicial branch is dependent upon the executive branch for enforcing their decrees. The courts simply do not possess any means to coerce compliance with their decisions without the assistance of the other two branches.

Most members of the judiciary agree with this circumscribed view of their political power and are willing to defer to the remaining two branches of government to solve society's problems. Not all judges agree with this restrained position, and throughout the history of the Supreme Court there have been brief periods when a group of like-thinking activist judges combine to dominate the Court and impatiently tackle some issues that have perplexed other branches of government. Fortunately for Ernest Miranda, he brought his federal appeal to the Supreme Court when it was in one of these periods and was willing to resolve important constitutional problems that had been ignored by the other two branches. The *Miranda* case arose at a time when activist justices were creating what journalist Fred Graham termed the due process revolution in which the Court paid special attention to a large number of cases involving the rights of persons accused of crimes. Similar to Ernest Miranda, these people had suffered at the hand of various state court systems and now turned to the highest federal court to declare that the due process clause of the Fourteenth Amendment had been violated during their initial trial and subsequent conviction.

Chapter 4

THE LEGAL PRECEDENTS

The American legal system is indebted to England, not only for passing along its tradition of providing basic rights to all citizens—first enunciated in the Magna Carta in 1215 and expanded in succeeding centuries—but even more basically for passing on its common-law system of judicial decision making. In contrast to nearly every other nation in the world, the United States and England rely upon their courts to develop the law on a case-by-case basis rather than the more typical codified systems derived from early Roman models. The common-law system is not without its problems, as law professor Craig Bradley observes:

> *Because of a unique constitutional system, America has developed its rules of criminal procedure piecemeal, on a case by case basis, rather than through a code of criminal procedure. Every other major country in the*

world uses a legislatively enacted code of criminal procedure. Only the United States expects its police to follow a set of rules so cumbersome and so complex, that one area of criminal procedure law alone—search and seizure—requires a four-volume treatise to explicate it.[1]

In the United States, although statutes and constitutions provide general guidelines, judges rely primarily upon earlier decisions on similar issues. This judicial doctrine is termed stare decisis, from the Latin phrase meaning "to stand by what has been decided." Although the earlier rulings are not inflexible rules from which a judge can never deviate, as Justice Louis Brandeis wrote: "Anglo-American law is built on the expectation that courts generally will follow what they have said in the past, on that assumption contracts are signed, wills made, lives planned."[2] Brandeis, however, does go on to qualify the long-term power of earlier precedents by pointing out that "in cases involving the Federal constitution, where correction through legislative action is practically impossible, this Court [the U.S. Supreme Court] has often overruled its earlier decisions. The court bows to the lessons of experience and the force of better reasoning."[3]

Because of the Supreme Court's traditional reliance on precedents, the lawyers for both Ernest Miranda and the State of Arizona spent many hours researching and analyzing previous Supreme Court decisions relevant to the *Miranda* case. Each side hoped to find support for their arguments in these decisions.

Initially the Supreme Court reviewed involuntary confessions in a manner consistent with traditional English common-law principles, which banned the use of such evidence because of its questionable reliability. The Supreme Court, however, went beyond this rationale and added a second reason for excluding this untrustworthy evidence. By the early twentieth century the Court had decided that the use of coerced confessions also undermined the government's ability to provide defendants with a fair trial and to treat them with the necessary degree of human decency—the broad requirements encompassed by the due process clause. Because the Fourteenth Amendment required due process of law before a state could deprive an individual of his or her life or liberty, the Supreme Court was, after ratification of the amendment in 1868, able to review state criminal convictions in which the police may have exceeded their authority and acted unconstitutionally in their efforts to obtain a confession. With this constitutional and historical background in mind, now let's take a look at the Supreme Court decisions that provide the critical precedents for the *Miranda* decision.

FIFTH AMENDMENT AND COERCED CONFESSIONS

In writing their briefs and preparing their oral arguments, Ernest Miranda's lawyers, John Flynn and John Paul Frank, and the lawyers for the state of Arizona closely examined Supreme Court decisions related to the Fifth Amendment and self-incrimination. It was apparent by the middle of the twentieth century that the Supreme Court was developing two policy objectives with regard to coerced confessions. In his book *The Supreme Court and Confessions of Guilt*, law professor Otis Stephens described the first objective as an effort to control extreme police brutality, both physical and psychological. This aim grew out of a series of cases during the 1930s and

1940s in which poor, vulnerable African-American defendants were victims of police brutality. Stephens wrote that "while police methods disclosed by such cases received the sharp condemnation of an aroused Supreme Court, primary attention was limited to the protection of individual defendants through the maintenance of elemental procedural standards at the trial level."[4]

The Court's second objective grew out of the undesirable police tactics that produced involuntary confessions. Beginning with the *McNabb* and *Mallory* cases, the Court developed, according to Stephens, "an elaborate set of interrogation requirements focusing on routine police conduct rather than on isolated examples of coercion."[5]

It is interesting to note that cases involving the Fifth Amendment and coerced confessions did not begin to reach the Supreme Court until the 1890s. Prior to this period, judicial officers, or magistrates, conducted the questioning of defendants prior to trial. It was not until the latter part of the nineteenth century that they turned over the interrogation responsibilities to the local police. Law professor Stephen Markham describes this transfer of responsibility: "The preliminary examination or hearing, which had previously been the essential vehicle for obtaining information from suspects was transformed into an optional proceeding, at which the defendant could avail himself the opportunity to respond to the charges against him, but was under no pressure to do so. The focus of interrogation moved from the courthouse to the station house."[6]

As noted in chapter 3, the early consequences of this shift from the courts to the police were not always positive. The Wickersham Report of 1931, as well as several other state and local investigative commissions, documented brutal police tactics designed to elicit confessions. The Courts, however, retained the power to decide whether the police had obtained a confession "voluntarily." In attempting to determine whether a confession satisfied the standard of voluntariness, the reviewing judge would examine "both the nature of the defendant and his circumstances, and the character of the police methods employed. If the confession was deemed to be 'voluntary' it was admitted into evidence, but if 'involuntary' it was excluded."[7]

The Fifth Amendment protects defendants in criminal cases from being compelled to be a witness against themselves. Unfortunately, as noted in chapter 3, this protection applies only to federal courts. The Court handed down its first ruling on the issue of confessions in 1884. In *Hopt v. Utah*, the Court defined a confession as involuntary if it "appears to have been made either in consequence of inducements of a temporal nature or because of a threat or promise . . . which, operating upon the fears or hopes of the accused . . . deprives him of that freedom of will or self-control essential to make his confession voluntary within the meaning of the law."[8]

The Court broadened its definition of voluntariness thirteen years later in *Bram v. U.S.* (1897). Its more expansive interpretation involved a statement made by a sailor accused of murder at sea. The Court held that in every case where a confession was being challenged the judge must consider "the circumstances surrounding and the facts established to exist, in reference to the confession in order to determine whether it was shown to have been made voluntarily."[9]

One of the primary factors that the federal courts viewed as critical in determining whether a confession had been made voluntarily was the amount of delay in charging a suspect with a crime.

By the 1940s several federal laws were enacted that required arresting officers to take an accused person promptly to a magistrate after he or she had been arrested. The Supreme Court gave its support to these laws, ruling in a 1943 case that confessions obtained after "unnecessary delay" in a suspect's arraignment could not be used as evidence in a federal court. In this case, *McNabb v. U.S.*, the Court overturned the conviction of several men who had murdered a federal revenue agent but had been subjected to three days of intensive questioning by federal prosecutors, without the assistance of any legal counsel, before they had been formally charged with the crime. The opinion, written by Justice Felix Frankfurter, was based upon the Court's supervisory powers to ensure the proper functioning of the federal judicial system rather than the Fifth Amendment's right against self-incrimination. Frankfurter explained that by prohibiting unnecessary delay between arrest and arraignment, courts are able to prevent "those reprehensible practices known as the 'third degree' which though universally rejected as indefensible, still find their way into use. It aims to avoid all the evil implications of secret interrogation of persons accused of crime. It reflects not a sentimental but a sturdy view of law enforcement. It outlaws easy but self-defeating ways in which brutality is substituted for brains as an instrument of crime detection."[10]

A few years later Congress enacted the Federal Rules of Criminal Procedure, which incorporated the holding in the *McNabb* decision. The Court reaffirmed its *McNabb* ruling in the case of *Mallory v. U.S.* (1957), nullifying a death sentence imposed upon a rapist whose confession came after more than eighteen hours between his arrest and arraignment. The resulting McNabb-Mallory rule indicated that "unnecessary delay" alone was a sufficient basis for excluding incriminating statements.

Congress, reflecting public displeasure with what was viewed as an excessive restraint upon police interrogations, limited the McNabb-Mallory rule through legislation. In the 1968 Omnibus Crime Control and Safe Streets Act, Congress enacted a rule in section 3501 (c) that a confession by a person in custody cannot be excluded solely because of delay in bringing the person before a magistrate if the confession is made within six hours of the arrest.[11]

At the time of the *Miranda* case, the McNabb-Mallory rule made things clearer when federal law officers obtained confessions, but what about applying the Fifth Amendment to state criminal cases, in which the great preponderance of local law enforcement interrogations were being reviewed by courts? As discussed in chapter 3, because of our federal system of government, state defendants are not protected by the Bill of Rights, which for our purposes means the Fifth Amendment privilege against compelled self-incrimination. We did learn, however, that through the passage of the Fourteenth Amendment, states cannot deny anyone life or liberty without due process of law. Therefore, the Supreme Court, long before it decided in *Molloy v. Hogan* (1964) to apply the Fifth Amendment to the states, used its rather vague supervisory responsibility under the Fourteenth Amendment to guarantee basic fairness in state criminal proceedings.

The first significant Supreme Court decision to overturn a state conviction because it was obtained by using an involuntary confession was the landmark case of *Brown v. Mississippi* (1936). The confessions from the African-American defendants in *Brown* resulted from beatings and death threats. In

*Chief Justice Charles Evans Hughes delivered
the ruling in* Brown v. Mississippi *(1936), the first
significant Supreme Court decision to strike down
a state criminal conviction because it was obtained
by using an involuntary confession.*

his majority opinion Chief Justice Charles Evans Hughes based his decision upon the conduct of the police, which violated the Fourteenth Amendment's due process requirements. Hughes saw a clear distinction between "compulsion" forbidden by the Fifth Amendment and "compulsion" forbidden by the Fourteenth Amendment's due process clause. He explained that:

> *The compulsion to which the . . . [Fifth Amendment] refer[s] is that of the processes of justice by which the accused may be called as a witness and required to testify. Compulsion by torture to extort a confession is a different matter. . . . Because a state may dispense with a jury trial, it does not follow that it may substitute trial by ordeal. The rack and torture chamber may not be substituted for the witness stand. . . . It would be difficult to conceive of methods more revolting to the sense of justice than those taken to procure the confessions of these petitioners, and the use of the confessions thus obtained as the basis for conviction and sentence was a clear denial of due process.*[12]

The following description of the facts in *Brown* clearly portrays the horrendous circumstance under which the confessions were obtained by the police. Hughes writes that:

> *The crime with which these defendants . . . are charged, was discovered about one o'clock P.M. on Friday, March 30, 1934. On that night one Dial, a deputy sheriff, accompanied by others, came to the home of Ellington, one of the defendants, and requested him to accompany them to the house of the deceased, and*

there a number of white men were gathered, who began to accuse the defendant of the crime. Upon his denial they seized him, and with the participation of the deputy they hanged him by a rope to the limb of a tree, and having let him down, they hung him again, and when he was let down the second time, and he still protested his innocence, he was tied to a tree and whipped, and still declining to accede to the demands that he confess, he was finally released and he returned with some difficulty to his home, suffering intense pain and agony. The record of the testimony shows that the signs of the rope on his neck were plainly visible during the so-called trial. A day or two thereafter the said deputy, accompanied by another, returned to the home of the said defendant and arrested him and departed with the prisoner towards the jail in an adjoining county, but went by a route which led into the State of Alabama; and while on the way, in that State, the deputy stopped and again severely whipped the defendant, declaring that he would continue the whipping until he confessed, and the defendant then agreed to confess to such a statement as the deputy would dictate, and he did so, after which he was delivered to jail.

The other two defendants, Ed Brown and Henry Shields, were also arrested and taken to the same jail. On Sunday night, April 1, 1934, the same deputy, accompanied by a number of white men, one of whom was also an officer, and by the jailer, came to the jail, and the two last named defendants were made to strip and they were laid over chairs and their backs were cut to pieces with a leather strap with buckles on it, and they were likewise made by the said deputy definitely to understand that the whipping would be continued unless and until they confessed, and not only confessed, but confessed in every matter of detail as demanded by those present; and in this manner the defendants confessed the crime, and as the whippings progressed and were repeated, they changed or adjusted their confession in all particulars of detail so as to conform to the demands of their torturers. When the confessions had been obtained in the exact form and contents as desired by the mob, they left with the parting admonition and warning that, if the defendants changed their story at any time in any respect from that last stated, the perpetrators of the outrage would administer the same or equally effect treatment.[13]

The Supreme Court continued to review carefully confessions in state criminal proceedings, and four years after *Brown* it ruled that psychological coercion, as well as physical torture, would not be permitted. In *Chambers v. Florida* (1940) four African-American men had been held incommunicado for several days and continually interrogated. The Supreme Court overturned their convictions stating that psychological coercion could produce involuntary confessions that violated the due process clause. Justice Black, writing the Court's opinion, declared:

The determination to preserve an accused's right to procedural due process sprang in large part from knowledge of the historical truth that the rights and liberties of people

*accused of crime could not be safely entrusted
to secret inquisitorial processes. . . .*

*For five days petitioners were subjected to
interrogations culminating in . . . [an] all
night examination. Over a period of five days
they steadily refused to confess and dis-
claimed any guilt. The very circumstances
surrounding their confinement and their
questioning without any formal charges having been brought, were such as to fill petitioners with terror and frightful misgivings. Some
were practically strangers in the community.
. . . The haunting fear of mob violence was
around them in an atmosphere charged with
excitement and public indignation. . . . To permit human lives to be forfeited upon confessions thus obtained would make of the
constitutional requirement of due process of
law a meaningless symbol. . . .*

*Due process of law, preserved for all by
our Constitution, commands that no such
practice as that disclosed by this record shall
send any accused to his death.*[14]

Although defense attorneys and civil libertarians
were encouraged by the *Chambers* decision, it did
little to clarify exactly what the Supreme Court
meant by "voluntariness." The Court continued to
confront the problems of coercive police practices for
the next twenty-five years, but it offered little in the
way of clear-cut standards for trial court judges in
evaluating confessions. Law professor Monrad
Paulsen summarized the Court's position in 1954,
writing that "the Federal confessions rule would be
used to discourage illegal police practices and not
simply to guard against erroneous convictions. But
none of the opinions had precisely defended the interrogation practices which were forbidden."[15]

The Supreme Court may have hoped that another governmental institution at either the federal or, more plausibly, the state level would declare statutorily what standards of voluntariness the police were to follow. Even today, most states have no code specifying the acceptable conduct of police interrogations. Without such a guideline, the Court between the *Brown* (1936) and *Miranda* (1966) decisions simply applied the ambiguous due process standards on a case-by-case basis. Stephen Markham describes the variety of strategies taken by the Supreme Court during this thirty-year period as it attempted to control police interrogation practices:

> *In the general approach that emerged, the intensity of the pressures to which the suspect had been subjected, and the factors relevant to his capacity to resist such pressures, were taken into account in order to determine whether he had been deprived of the capacity for choice in making the confession. Factors relating to the method of interrogation that weighed against a finding of voluntariness and admissibility included physical abuse, threats of violence, relentlessly protracted and repeated interrogation, questioning during lengthy periods of unlawful detention, deprivation of food and sleep, and isolation of the suspect. Characteristics of the suspect that weighed in the same direction included youth, lack of education or intelligence, membership in a racial minority, poverty, and psychological disabilities. The fact that a suspect was unaware of, or had not been advised of his rights, and denial of access to counsel, were also noted in a number of cases, but only as two factors among many others bearing on the general determination of voluntariness.*[16]

By the mid-1960s several new justices had been added to the Court. A change in the Court's attitude toward the rights of defendants accused in state criminal proceedings was readily apparent as "the due process revolution" moved toward its zenith. The decision in *Gideon v. Wainwright* (1963), which elevated the Sixth Amendment's right to counsel to all defendants in both federal and state criminal cases, is an example of this development. It was clear that by the time it was considering the *Miranda* case, the Court was not only willing to take an activist position and disregard earlier precedents but it was also favorably disposed toward creating uniform federal standards of criminal procedure.

This willingness to exercise its authority and intrude into what was formerly the province of state and local criminal justice systems was evident in the Supreme Court's decision in *Molloy v. Hogan* (1964). In this case the Court decided to eliminate the confusion over whether coerced confessions in state criminal proceedings were a due process and fair trial question by incorporating the Fifth Amendment through the Fourteenth Amendment. Thus, all violations of the Fifth Amendment right against self-incrimination, however minor, would result in a state court excluding the confession as evidence in trial. The privilege against self-incrimination had finally been elevated to that honor roll of fundamental freedoms that Justice Benjamin Cardozo had characterized as "implicit in the concept of ordered liberty."[17]

CONFESSIONS AND THE RIGHT TO COUNSEL: IMMEDIATE PRECEDENTS FOR *MIRANDA*

We have seen that confessions are typically made by defendants in the somewhat hostile environment of police stations. The accused is forced to withstand the questioning in isolation, without the assistance of counsel. No one is likely to have informed him or her of their Fifth Amendment rights to remain silent and not incriminate himself or herself. By linking the presence of an attorney to pretrial interrogations, it can be assumed that defendants have received sound advice concerning whether it is in their best interests to answer the police officer's questions or to simply employ their constitutional right to remain silent and not cooperate.

A year before the Supreme Court incorporated the Fifth Amendment right against self-incrimination to the states through the Fourteenth Amendment in *Molloy*, it decided in *Gideon v. Wainwright* (1963) that any defendant in a state criminal proceeding had a right to an attorney and that if he or she could not afford one the state would provide counsel at no cost. Although the Court in *Gideon* narrowed the holding of its decision to the issue of guaranteeing counsel at the defendant's trial, the broader question of how much earlier in the proceedings did a defendant have a right to an attorney was left unanswered. By linking the right to counsel issue with the coerced confession problem, *Miranda* raised the question of whether the Supreme Court would extend this attorney coverage to the earliest pretrial period in which the defendant is arrested and brought into custody. A closely related problem, also raised by *Miranda*, is whether the police are under constitutional obligation to notify the defendant of his or her right to counsel at this initial point of arrest and confinement.

Prior to the *Gideon* decision, the Supreme Court appeared reluctant to provide very clear guidelines for the police and lower courts on any of these related right-to-counsel and coerced confessions issues. *Crooker v. California* (1958) is typical of the way in which the Supreme Court addressed these problems during this period. In *Crooker*, the Court split 5–4 in deciding that the denial of an attorney during police questioning did not violate the rights of a defendant who had a college degree and some law school training. Yet in the following year in *Spano v. New York*, the Court unanimously agreed that an attorney was required for a defendant who had confessed after an early morning interrogation by the police.[18]

Two decisions, *Massiah v. U.S.* and *Escobedo v. Illinois*, which were decided in 1964, just one year after *Gideon*, set the stage for the *Miranda* decision. Both of these cases were most instructive in clarifying when a defendant's right-to-counsel protections began and how closely this Sixth Amendment protection was linked to the Fifth Amendment's privilege against self-incrimination.

The first case, *Massiah v. U.S.*, involved two defendants accused of trafficking narcotics and laid the groundwork for *Escobedo,* which was decided later that same term. Winston Massiah had been arraigned, released on bail, and had even retained a lawyer. His codefendant, however, decided to become a government informer and tricked Massiah into making several incriminating statements, which the prosecution used to convict him. The Supreme Court held that Massiah's Fifth and Sixth Amendment rights were violated. Writing the majority opinion for the Court, Justice Potter Stewart declared that the statements were inadmissible under the Sixth Amendment because the accused did not enjoy the assistance of counsel at the time he uttered his damning statements.

Although Justice Stewart's opinion was a narrow one focusing on the unique circumstances of Massiah's case, the case nevertheless established the precedent that voluntary confessions can be excluded by the Court for failure of the police to respect a defendant's right of counsel prior to trial. In his book on the Warren Court's due process revolution, journalist Fred Graham summarized the significance of the *Massiah* decision: "Nothing goes quite as abrasively against the grain of lawyer's thinking than efforts by one side of a controversy to go behind the opposing attorney's back to weaken his case through direct contacts with his client. In civil litigation it can lead to settlements that threaten the wronged attorneys' fees as well as the strength of their cases, and judges, having been lawyers themselves, consider it impropriety of the highest order. In Massiah's case the Supreme Court found it no less than a breach of the Sixth Amendment's declaration that 'in all criminal prosecutions, the accused shall enjoy the right to have the assistance of counsel for his defense.'"[19] Thus, the *Massiah* case is significant because it was the first time the Court had stretched the right to counsel to the pretrial stage of police interrogation, and on an even broader issue, it indicated the Supreme Court's newfound willingness to improve policy decisions in the guise of constitutional interpretation.

A few days after both the *Molloy* and *Massiah* decisions were handed down, the U.S. Supreme Court in *Escobedo v. Illinois* established the final precedent that became a cornerstone in *Miranda v. Arizona*. This case would move the Sixth Amendment right to counsel from the courthouse, as established in *Gideon*, to the station house. The case involved a scrawny, sociopathic youngster named Danny Escobedo. He had been a thorn in the side of the Chicago police since he was a juvenile, and as a result of his criminal experiences, he was sufficiently street-smart to have a lawyer on call when he was arrested. Escobedo this time had been accused of murdering his brother-in-law. He was arrested by

Justice Potter Stewart wrote the majority opinion in Massiah v. U.S. *(1964), a case that established the precedent that the Supreme Court could invalidate a voluntary confession if the police failed to respect a defendant's right of counsel before the trial stage.*

the police and brought into the station house where they began questioning him. Escobedo on several occasions asked for his attorney to be present, but the police denied his requests. The police detained the lawyer outside the interrogation room while they continued their questioning. They told Escobedo that an accomplice had blamed the whole incident on him. Escobedo caved into the police trickery—the accomplice had not told the police anything—and admitted that he had been involved. He insisted that the accomplice had been the trigger man. Detectives continued to wring out a confession that led to Escobedo's conviction.

In a narrow 5–4 decision, Justice Arthur Goldberg wrote the majority opinion. For the first time the Supreme Court abandoned the ambiguous and confusing voluntarism standard for determining the admissibility of confessions and instead emphasized the procedures followed by the police in obtaining the confession. Justice Goldberg explained the essence of the Court's holding in *Escobedo*:

> *We hold . . . that where, as here, the investigation is no longer a general inquiry into an unsolved crime but has begun to focus on a particular suspect, the suspect has been taken into police custody, the police carry out a process of interrogations that lend itself to eliciting incriminating statements, the suspect has requested and been denied an opportunity to consult with his lawyer, and the police have not effectively warned him of his absolute constitutional right to remain silent, the accused has been denied "the Assistance of Counsel" in violation of the Sixth Amendment to the Constitution as "made obligatory upon the States by the Fourteenth Amendment,"*

*and that no statement elicited by the police
during the interrogation may be used against
him at a criminal trial.*[20]

The reaction of law enforcement officials and many
legal scholars was immediate and angry. Never before had the police had to worry about having a defense attorney available in order to validate or
sanctify actions taken in the station house or the interrogation room. A strong proponent of law enforcement authority, Fred Inbau of Northwestern
University Law School stated that the *Escobedo* decision was "the hardest body blow the court has
struck yet against enforcement of law in this nation."[21] The case also made law enforcement officials
nervous because of the specter of where future cases,
which would use *Escobedo* as a jumping-off point,
might go. Suppose a defendant did not have a
lawyer? What if no actual request had been made?
Did the police have a constitutional obligation to inform the defendant of his or her Sixth Amendment
rights? And what about the defendants' related
rights under the Fifth Amendment to remain silent
and not incriminate themselves? Would the police
also have to inform all defendants of this right?
Fred Graham of the *New York Times* summarized what happened next in his book *The Self-In-
flicted Wound*:

> *The Supreme Court had been expected to let
> these and other questions simmer for years in
> the lower courts, where various solutions
> could be tested and modified. . . . But events
> forced another course. Appeals flooded the
> lower courts. Most of them stood pat on Es-
> cobedo and passed the cases up to the
> Supreme Court for further amplification. By*

In this photo, Danny Escobedo is detained by police in 1966 after being charged with the burglary of a hot dog stand. Escobedo had been freed from jail two years earlier when the U.S. Supreme Court overturned his 1963 murder conviction because the police had refused to let him consult his lawyer before he confessed to killing his brother-in-law. The Court's decision in Escobedo v. Illinois *(1964) was an important precedent in* Miranda v. Arizona.

the autumn of 1965 the Court had decided to answer all of the questions at once, to undertake a broad rule-making hearing unlike anything that had ever occurred before in a court of the United States . . . to frame broad legislative codes to cover future police conduct.[22]

Thus, Ernest Miranda was about to make constitutional history. His ill-fated encounter with the Phoenix police department would be one of those four cases the Supreme Court decided to hear in the fall of 1965 in the hopes of resolving the many unanswered questions raised by the *Escobedo* decision.

AMICUS CURIAE BRIEFS
In a case that raises important legal and emotional issues and appears likely to become a landmark decision, such as *Miranda v. Arizona*, various interest groups representing divergent points of view attempt to influence the Supreme Court's decision by submitting amicus curiae briefs supporting one of the contesting parties. Underlying the practice of amicus briefs was the belief that organizations could assist the Court in providing expertise and experience beyond the capacity of the adversaries. By the time of *Miranda*, however, amicus briefs served simply as an indicator of public support for one side or the other. Because there is the potential for the Supreme Court to be flooded in a highly controversial case such as *Miranda*, the Court enacted a requirement that amicus briefs could only be filed with the consent of all parties to the case. A major exception to this rule, however, and of relevance to this case, is that the federal government and any state government always have the opportunity to file an amicus brief.

In *Miranda v. Arizona*, the American Civil Liberties Union was the only group that filed a brief in support of Miranda. The organization had long been associated with defendants' rights and consistently advocated an activist position by the Supreme Court in order to guarantee due process, especially for those facing criminal charges in state courts. Two groups filed briefs endorsing the position of the State of Arizona: the National District Attorney's Association and the attorney general of New York, who was joined by the attorneys general of twenty-six additional states. These briefs emphasized the expected negative impact of the decision if the Court ruled in favor of Miranda. They argued that law enforcement officers would face serious handicaps in their ability to interrogate suspects and become even further hampered in their already frustrating and seemingly losing battle with society's criminal element. Assessing the impact of the National District Attorney's Association amicus briefs, Fred Graham concluded:

> *The National District Attorney's Association had submitted scattered statistics from various members, showing that confessions had been a helpful tool of their trade. Since much had been made of the fact that warnings were already required in England in the form of the Judges' Rules, they compared the reported crime rates to point out such revealing contrasts as England's robbery rate of 6.5 per 100,000 people, as against Chicago's rate of 273.9 per 100,000—which to them suggested caution in saddling U.S. law enforcement with tighter interrogation than those in effect in England. (Soon after, a move began in England to relax the restrictions on police interrogation on the ground that the crime rate was alarmingly high.) But the Supreme Court had been confronted with scare statis-*

tics before and had found them less reliable than its own instincts for reform, and some of the Justices made it clear during the Miranda *arguments that* Escobedo *had made these arguments irrelevant.*[23]

Graham's comments raise the broader question of how important are these amicus briefs in terms of influencing the Supreme Court's decision. It is very difficult to answer this question, and research has been both scarce and inconclusive. In the next chapter we will examine how these groups join with the primary adversaries to present their position during the oral argument stage.

Chapter 5
THE COURT DECIDES

It was a gray Monday morning, the last day of February 1966. Ernest Miranda's lawyer, John Flynn arrived early at the Supreme Court building in Washington, D.C. (John Paul Frank, although senior appellate attorney at Lewis and Roca, decided to defer to Flynn because of Flynn's superior firsthand experience in criminal law and Phoenix police practices.) Not only was Flynn prepared to present his client's case in oral argument before the Court that day, but Chief Justice Earl Warren was scheduled to swear him in as a new member of the Supreme Court bar. Following this brief ceremonial proceeding, the Court would begin hearing that day's oral arguments. Each side in *Miranda v. Arizona* would be given a half hour to argue its position before the justices.

ORAL ARGUMENT
The oral argument stage of a Supreme Court proceeding occurs approximately four months after the

Court has agreed to review a case. During this period, counsel for each side and those groups that are granted amicus status carefully prepare their written briefs and oral presentations. Because the justices typically interrupt the presentations with their own questions, the lawyers must be prepared to answer any question about the issues in the case.

How important is this oral argument phase in affecting the final outcome of a Supreme Court case? Chief Justice Charles Evans Hughes wrote that the significance of the oral argument is a direct by-product of the fact that often "the impression that a judge has at the close of a full oral argument accords with the conviction which controls his final vote."[1] Because the oral arguments are usually held Monday through Wednesday and the justices vote on the case a day or two later during that week's conference, many justices have agreed with Justice William Brennan that the oral arguments come at a crucial time and "on many occasions . . . my judgment or a decision has turned on what happened in oral argument."[2] Justice Lewis Powell further clarifies the oral arguments' importance by explaining, "The fact is that the quality of advocacy—the research, briefing and oral argument of the close and difficult cases—does contribute significantly to the development of precedents."[3]

One of the most interesting aspects of the oral argument is that it provides an impression about the direction each justice is likely to go in deciding the case. Although a few justices may do little to tip their hands through friendly or hostile treatment of the opposing counsel, the *Miranda* case was of such importance that nearly all of the justices actively participated in the oral arguments and provided a clear indication of their forthcoming vote. The sole exception was Justice Brennan, who remained relatively silent.

Because three other cases involving interrogation issues were heard at the same time,[4] along with the arguments of numerous amicus curiae advocates, the oral arguments phase stretched to three full days. John Flynn faced not only Gary Nelson, the young assistant attorney general arguing for the State of Arizona, but also such highly respected and nationally renowned attorneys as law professor Telford Taylor, arguing as amicus for the attorneys general of twenty-seven states, and U.S. Solicitor Thurgood Marshall, arguing on behalf of the U.S. Department of Justice. A former civil-rights lawyer and a future Supreme Court justice renowned for his liberal stances, Marshall found himself in the unusual position of arguing against expanding the rights of those accused of crimes.

Despite what he later confessed to be a feeling of intense nervousness, John Flynn strode to the lectern and in a firm, steady voice presented what he believed to be the major thrust of his case: that the Court must exclude Miranda's confession based upon the Fifth Amendment's prohibition against a defendant's being compelled to incriminate himself rather than simply the Sixth Amendment's right to counsel. He had barely completed summarizing the facts of the case when the justices began their questioning.

Justice Fortas went first, and it soon became apparent that he supported Flynn's position and even went so far as to suggest that the case should be viewed "in terms of the great human adventure towards some kind of truly civilized order . . . what we are dealing with here is not just the criminal in society but it is the problem of the relationship of the state and the individual, in the large and philosophical sense, viewed in the light of the total history of mankind, part of that being the Magna Carta and the Bill of Rights."[5]

Flynn concluded his allotted half hour with an effort to refute the argument that the various state legislatures should be allowed a chance to solve the problem of protecting defendants' rights in the police station. Flynn pointed out that:

> *The constitution of the State of Arizona . . . has in statehood provided to the citizens of our state language precisely the same as the 4th Amendment to the Federal Constitution as it pertains to searches and seizures, yet, from 1914 until this Court's decision in* Mapp versus Ohio, *we simply did not enjoy the . . . Amendment rights that were enjoyed by most of the other citizens of the other states of this union. . . . [Should solution of the confessions problem be left again to the states] it would be another 46 years before the 6th Amendment right in the scope that it was intended, I submit, by this court in* Escobedo *will reach the State of Arizona.*[6]

Sensing the Court's acceptance of Flynn's argument, a nervous Gary Nelson, likewise making his first appearance before the U.S. Supreme Court, quickly launched into his argument that the *Miranda* case was more of a Sixth Amendment right-to-counsel case than a Fifth Amendment self-incrimination case. The essence of his position was that the Court should slow down and not go beyond the recent *Escobedo* decision. Nelson tried to assume a reasonable position, one clearly opposing brutal, coercive police

Gary Nelson, a state assistant attorney general, represented the State of Arizona in the oral arguments of Miranda v. Arizona. *Nelson warned the Supreme Court that if it expanded the protections given to those accused of crimes, as proposed by Miranda's attorney, the Court would significantly hamper the ability of law enforcement officials to fight crime.*

conduct but asserting that most police officers acted in a civilized manner. He forcefully closed his argument with a statement that reflected the fears of most law enforcement officers in the event the Court expanded the protections given to the accused under *Escobedo*:

> *I think if the extreme position is adopted that says he has to either have counsel at this stage or intelligently waive counsel, that a serious problem in the enforcement of our criminal law will occur. First of all, let us make one thing certain [he told the justices speaking more slowly now, letting them absorb the full significance]. We need no empirical data as to one factor, what counsel will do if he is actually introduced. . . . At least among lawyers there can be no doubt as to what counsel for the defendant is supposed to be doing. He is to represent him 100 percent, win, lose or draw, guilty or innocent. That is our system. When counsel is introduced at an interrogation, interrogation ceases immediately.*[7]

It was now time for the illustrious attorneys Telford Taylor, Thurgood Marshall, and Duane Nedrud, executive director of the National District Attorney's Association, to argue from their amicus curiae positions in support of the State of Arizona. During their presentations other members of the Court made their positions clear through the tone of their questioning. Chief Justice Earl Warren, who had been a former prosecutor and personally observed questionable station house practices, made it clear that he was strongly committed to increasing the rights of persons under interrogation. Fred Graham, in his

*As solicitor general, Thurgood Marshall,
pictured here in 1960, argued in support of
the State of Arizona in* Miranda v. Arizona.

book *The Due Process Revolution*, described Warren's thought process:

> *Warren often saw great constitutional issues in intensely personal terms. A decade before, he had been outraged by press reports of a "dragnet arrest" incident in Washington, in which policemen in search of three "stocky" Negro robbery suspects rounded up ninety youths who seemed to match the description—and ultimately charged someone not among the ninety. In criminal cases that came to the Supreme Court after that, states' attorneys learned to dread the Dragnet Story, for if Warren told it during the oral arguments, he was certain to vote for the accused. Early in the* Miranda *arguments he related the Dragnet Story in vivid detail, telling how "the police went out to a certain area of the city and gathered up 90—not 9 but 90—people who might answer that description, knocked them out of bed, and threw them into jail and didn't process them by morning."*[8]

THE CONFERENCE

By the end of the prolonged oral argument stage, the Court had learned all of the factual details of the *Miranda* case, as well as the philosophical and pragmatic arguments of both sides. The questioning of the attorneys had been dominated by Chief Justice Warren and justices Black, Stewart, and Fortas. As John Flynn and Gary Nelson left the courtroom on Wednesday afternoon, they both felt that the Court had already made up its mind.

On Friday, October 4, the justices met in their customary private conference to discuss and vote upon the cases heard in oral argument earlier in the week. This private conference is held in a small room, and great care is taken to ensure that all discussions and votes are kept secret. Justice Powell explained the necessity of maintaining a high level of secrecy, writing "the integrity of decision-making would be impaired seriously if we had to reach our judgments in the atmosphere of an ongoing town meeting. There must be candid discussion, a willingness to consider arguments advanced by other Justices, and a continuing examination and reexamination of one's own views."[9]

To ensure secrecy, no written record is kept of the proceedings, and each justice is restricted to bringing only a small notebook for recording his or her vote on that day's scheduled cases. In earlier times the conference discussions involved lengthy deliberations, but as the caseload increased the discussions grew more abbreviated. Today the conference serves primarily to discover consensus; there is little time to compromise or change someone's mind through an eloquent and persuasive argument. Justice Douglas noted that because of these time limitations, conference discussions rarely change a justice's position. It is generally agreed that the justices now come prepared to vote, having resolved their position through a review and analysis of each case scheduled for that week's conference.

Within a few days after the conference, a decision is made regarding which justice will write the majority opinion. If the chief justice is on the winning side, he or she has the power either to write the opinion himself or herself or to choose the author. If the chief justice is not on the winning side, then the most senior associate justice has the responsibility of either writing for the majority or choosing someone else. In *Miranda*, Chief Justice Warren decided to write the majority opinion. As was clear during the oral argument, he was very interested in the case and wanted to shape the Court's position.

Following the secret vote on a case and the selection of a justice to write the majority opinion, several months typically pass before the written decision is released to the public. During these months the justices circulate drafts of the majority opinion, as well as concurring and dissenting opinions that are written in reaction to the majority opinion. The secretive nature of the conference extends to this rather lengthy period before the Court's official opinion is released. (In the *Miranda* case it was approximately three and one-half months.) The Court has been remarkably successful in maintaining this veil of secrecy with only a handful of instances of premature leaks in the two-hundred-year history of the Court.

Because of the veil of secrecy, no one knows what transpires during the oral conference or throughout the period of time when opinions are being written. It has been learned, however, from the controversial book on the Supreme Court, *The Brethren*, by Bob Woodward and Scott Armstrong, that there is often a great deal of interaction between the justices during this period. The custom is to circulate opinions in a draft stage, which can generate discussion and even lobbying efforts to convince colleagues to join with or amend their opinion. Before a justice will officially sign on to a majority opinion or join with a colleague in a concurring or dissenting opinion, he or she will want to review the draft carefully. It is conceivable that on occasion justices have even switched sides, reversing their original vote as a result of subsequent discussions during these months. But, again, because of the secrecy and absence of any recorded debate, no one will ever be certain of what transpired in the course of the Court's deliberations on *Miranda*.

DELIVERING THE OPINION

Keeping with Supreme Court tradition, there was no prior announcement indicating when the Court would hand down its decision in *Miranda*. Ever since the oral argument in March, the press, legal scholars, prosecutors, defense attorneys, and judges had anxiously awaited the decision. Most believed that the Court would amend or possibly expand its recent *Escobedo* decision, but exactly how far and in what form perplexed everyone. Because word had leaked out that the opinion would be delivered Monday, June 13, along with the three other confession cases that had been argued along with *Miranda*, the Court was packed on that day. Chief Justice Warren, visibly sensing the importance of the moment, read the entire opinion, an unusually lengthy one that stretched to sixty pages. He spoke in a grave yet emotional voice for nearly an hour.

As reporters and other members of the audience quickly sensed, the chief justice was neither willing to wait for legislatures to clear up the problems of coerced station house confessions nor willing to rely on the good intentions of law enforcement officials to control themselves. The problems raised in *Escobedo* would have to be resolved by the Supreme Court.

The Court, however, would base its decision on the self-incrimination prohibition of the Fifth Amendment rather than the Sixth Amendment's right-to-counsel guarantee, which was the constitutional foundation of the *Escobedo* decision. Thus, Warren and other members of the majority thought it was more important to emphasize the coercive nature of station house interrogations than to emphasize the narrower, and in many ways less sensitive, issue of how soon and in what fashion a defendant's right to counsel was to begin.

The three other cases that were clustered under the *Miranda* umbrella are today forgotten by the general public. Nevertheless, they each contributed a factual situation that helped to clarify the scope of the opinion. The second sentence of the *Miranda* opinion clearly sets forth the constitutional thread that united all four cases: "we deal with the admissibility of statements obtained from an individual who is subjected to custodial police interrogation."[10] In *Miranda*, the defendant was picked up by two detectives at his home and taken into custody at a Phoenix police station, where he was identified by the complaining witness. After a two-hour interrogation, police officers emerged from the interrogation room with a signed confession. In the second case, *Vignera v. New York*, the defendant was picked up in connection with a robbery and transported to a detective squad headquarters. After being moved to another office, he was further interrogated and he confessed. Vignera was next transported to a lockup, and after eight more hours he gave the prosecutor a signed confession. The third case, *Westover v. U.S.*, involved the federal government, specifically the Federal Bureau of Investigation (FBI). The suspect was arrested by the Kansas City police for a local robbery. The FBI informed the department that the defendant was wanted in California on a serious felony charge. He was placed in a lineup and booked, then interrogated during the evening and again the next morning. The FBI conducted its interrogation the subsequent afternoon. After two hours, the defendant signed two confessions. All interrogations occurred in the same police station. The fourth and final case was *California v. Stewart*. The defendant was arrested in his home, where proceeds from a robbery were found. He was immediately taken to a police station and placed in a cell. Stewart was interrogated nine times over the next five days.

MAJORITY OPINION

In his opinion, which was joined by justices Douglas, Black, Brennan, and Fortas, Chief Justice Warren characterized the common features of all four cases: "In each, the defendant was questioned [by law enforcement officials] in a room in which he was cut off from the outside world. . . . They all thus share salient features—incommunicado interrogation of individuals in a police dominated atmosphere."[11] As Warren began reading the opening paragraphs of the opinion, it soon became clear to the expectant listeners crammed into the Court that warm spring morning that the opinion had the definitive tone of a statutory pronouncement. The chief justice explained:

> *Our holding will be spelled out with some specificity in the pages which follow but briefly stated it is this: the prosecution may not use statements, whether exculpatory or inculpatory, stemming from custodial interrogation of the defendant unless it demonstrates the use of procedural safeguards effective to secure the privilege against self-incrimination. By custodial interrogation, we mean questioning initiated by law enforcement officers after a person has been taken into custody or otherwise deprived of his freedom of action in any significant way. As for the procedural safeguards to be employed, unless other fully effective means are devised*

to inform accused persons of their right of silence and to assure a continuous opportunity to exercise it, the following measures are required. Prior to any questioning, the person must be warned that he has a right to remain silent, that any statement he does make may be used as evidence against him, and that he has a right to the presence of an attorney, either retained or appointed. The defendant may waive effectuation of these rights, provided the waiver is made voluntarily, knowingly and intelligently. If, however, he indicates in any manner and at any stage of the process that he wishes to consult with an attorney before speaking there can be no questioning. Likewise, if the individual is alone and indicates in any manner that he does not wish to be interrogated, the police may not question him. The mere fact that he may have answered some questions or volunteered some statement on his own does not deprive him of the right to refrain from answering any further inquiries until he has consulted with an attorney and thereafter consents to be questioned.[12]

In other words, the Court held that no statement made by an arrested person at a police station can be admitted as evidence against him or her unless certain factors were met at the station house. Before being questioned, the arrested person must have been told that he or she is not required to say anything, that anything he or she decides to say may be used against him or her at trial, that the defendent may consult with an attorney before and during the questioning, and that the state will provide him or her with an attorney if he or she cannot afford one.

Chief Justice Earl Warren delivered the Supreme Court's opinion in Miranda v. Arizona. *By a 5–4 vote, the deeply divided Court reversed Miranda's conviction because he had been interrogated without being informed of his right to remain silent and his right to an attorney. The Court ruled that statements made by suspects in police custody could not be used as evidence against them unless they had been informed of their Fifth Amendment right against self-incrimination and their Sixth Amendment right to legal counsel.*

Both judges and lawyers were immediately caught off guard by the sweeping declarations of the opening salvo of the decision. It was accepted Supreme Court practice to avoid making such broad, expansive statements because it made the Court appear to be a type of supralegislature. Warren and his supporters on the majority, especially Fortas and Douglas, were greatly troubled by the flood of appeals following the *Escobedo* decision. They sensed that *Miranda* was the proper vehicle for confronting the wide range of interrogation issues that resulted from the *Escobedo* decision. Moving cautiously on a narrow case-by-case basis and relying on the "critical stage" doctrine of the Sixth Amendment—which was the basis for determining precisely when the right to counsel begins to become effective—would not solve the inevitable flood of interrogation-related issues. It was time, the majority seemed to be asserting, to tackle the problem directly and resolve it with a statutory-like set of directives for law enforcement personnel to follow.

The chief justice, being a longtime political activist at both the state and national levels, was well aware that he had pushed the Court into a legislative posture. He acknowledged the awkwardness and even unpopularity of this position, writing, "We cannot say that the Constitution necessarily requires the adherence to any particular solution for the inherent compulsions of the interrogation process." He even went so far as to encourage state and federal governments to step in and formulate their own set of interrogation procedures, but he concluded that until they "implemented procedures which are at best as effective in apprising accused persons of their rights of silence and in assuring a continuous opportunity to exercise it, the rules announced today must be followed."[13]

In typical Supreme Court fashion, even when courageously setting down new and expansive interpretations of our constitutional rights, Warren wanted to assure both the legal community and the general public that this decision was not a sharp break with tradition or an irresponsible innovation. Rather, the Court was simply creating a contemporary application to long-standing principles and precedents. The chief justice devoted much time to citing earlier confession cases—such as *Chambers v. Florida, Blackburn v. Alabama, Haynes v. Washington,* and *Townsend v. Sain*—which provided support for the *Miranda* decision. All cases were cited to illustrate a common problem of psychological coercion and the necessity for the Court's diligent supervision of law enforcement excesses. Warren found that *Miranda* and the other three confession cases before the Court, as well as many earlier precedents, illustrate the inherently coercive atmosphere of police station interrogation and concluded that:

> *an interrogation environment is created for no purpose other than to subjugate the individual to the will of his examiner. This atmosphere carries its own badge of intimidation. To be sure, this is not physical intimidation, but it is equally destructive of human dignity. The current practice of incommunicado interrogation is at odds with one of our Nation's most cherished principles—that the individual may not be compelled to incriminate himself. Unless adequate protective devices are employed to dispel the compulsion inherent in custodial surroundings, no statement obtained from the defendant can truly be the product of his free choice.*[14]

Warren attempted to make clear that the Court was not prohibiting *all* statements obtained during interrogation. He emphasized, however, that if a statement is taken from a defendant without the presence of his or her attorney, then the government has a heavy burden to convince the Court that the defendant knowingly and intelligently waived the privilege against self-incrimination and the right to be represented by counsel. Warren concludes his opinion forcefully, arguing, "Since the State is responsible for establishing the isolated circumstances under which the interrogation takes place and has the only means of making available corroborated evidence of warnings given during incommunicado interrogation, the burden is rightly on its shoulders."[15]

The chief justice acknowledged that many Americans believe that society's general welfare requires and even outweighs the need to protect defendants from police interrogation. Warren declared his sensitivity to the policeman's difficult position of protecting the safety of society but reiterated that there are compelling reasons why a defendant's Fifth and Sixth Amendment due process rights cannot be compromised. He concluded section IV of the opinion by quoting one of Justice Brandeis's most eloquent statements (albeit part of a dissenting opinion) in *Olmstead v. U.S.* (1928):

> *Decency, security and liberty alike demand that government officials shall be subjected to the same rules of conduct that are commands to the citizen. In a government of laws, existence of the government will be imperiled if it fails to observe the law scrupulously. Our Government is the potent, the omnipresent teacher. For good or for ill, it teaches the*

whole people by its example. Crime is conta-gious. If the Government becomes a lawbreak-er, it breeds contempt for law; it invites every man to become a law unto himself; it invites anarchy. To declare that in the administra-tion of the criminal law the end justifies the means . . . would bring terrible retribution. Against that pernicious doctrine this Court should resolutely set its face.[16]

DISSENTING OPINIONS

The *Miranda* decision came from a closely divided Court. Several members were upset with the *Escobedo* decision, and they were even more cha-grined to see how the chief justice had expanded it in *Miranda*. Three of the four minority justices chose to write dissenting opinions, hoping to air their con-cern with the decision and share their feelings with the public. The roots of the dissenting opinions could first be seen in *Gideon v. Wainwright*. Although *Gideon* was a unanimous decision, the concurring opinions of justices Clark and Harlan expressed mild misgivings. Two years later in *Escobedo*, the four dissenters—Clark, Harlan, Stewart, and White—were sharp in their criticism. Now one year later these four justices again joined together as dis-senters in the *Miranda* case. They formed a coherent and cohesive group that believed their colleagues had gone too far in balancing the rights of defen-dants against the safety of society. They denied that the Fifth Amendment should be treated as an ab-solute and stated it should instead be interpreted with regard to both law enforcement and societal in-terests. If providing additional safeguards for sus-pects during their station house interrogation imposed a greater burden on police and prosecutors, these four justices wanted this burden to be considered in determining the scope of the applicable constitutional protections.

Tom Clark was the first justice to read his dissenting opinion. Having worked as a prosecutor and served as U.S. attorney general, the former law enforcement official had been a longtime defender of the police. Usually easygoing and gregarious, Justice Clark's voice had a noticeable edge when reading his dissent, which challenged the chief justice's assumptions and expressed his own confidence in local police. Clark believed that the police had been unjustifiably maligned by the majority opinion, which he thought had no basis in earlier decisions. Clark was especially troubled by Warren's persistent criticism of the police, inferring systematic wrongdoing that the law enforcement community was incapable of correcting. Moved to a rare show of emotion, Clark argued that it was unfair to "pillory the police over interrogation manuals written by law professors and rarely used by the police."[17] Still upset after completing the reading of his dissent, Clark took the unusual step of amending his opinion before sending it to the Government Printing Office for official publication in the *United States Reports*. Fred Graham reported that Clark had added the following phrase to the final version to clarify his position further:

> *The police agencies—all the way from municipal and state forces to the Federal bureau— are responsible for law enforcement and public safety in this country. I am proud of their efforts, which in my view are not fairly characterized by the Court's opinion.*[18]

A second dissenting opinion, written by Justice Harlan, was endorsed by justices White and Stewart. The first two sentences of Harlan's opinion presented the essence of his criticism: "I believe the decision of the Court represents poor constitutional law and entails harmful consequences for the country at large. How serious these consequences may prove to be only time can tell."[19] Harlan had written a strong one-paragraph dissent in *Escobedo*, charging the Court with unjustifiably hampering "the perfectly legitimate methods of criminal law enforcement." In *Miranda*, Harlan was even more concerned with the impact of the decision upon police effectiveness. He found Warren's rules to be "hasty and impulsive." He accused the majority of ignoring the fact that:

> *its rules impair, if they will not eventually serve to frustrate an instrument of law enforcement that has long and quite reasonably been thought worth the price paid for it. There can be little doubt that the Court's new code would markedly decrease the number of confessions. . . . How much harm this decision will inflict on law enforcement cannot fairly be predicted with accuracy. Evidence on the role of confessions is notoriously incomplete, . . . and little is added by the Court's reference to the FBI experience and the resources believed wasted in interrogation. . . . We do know that some crimes cannot be solved without confessions, that ample expert testimony attests to their importance in crime control, and that the Court is taking a real risk with society's welfare in imposing its new regime on the country. The social costs of crime are too great to call the new rules anything but a hazardous experimentation.*[20]

The final written dissent was delivered by Justice White, whose brief statements were joined in by justices Harlan and Stewart. Although an ardent civil rights advocate, White had surprised many Court

Justice Byron White was one of the four justices who disagreed with Warren's majority opinion in Miranda. In his dissenting opinion, White wrote that the majority decision had no support in the language of the Fifth Amendment.

observers with his consistently tough law-and-order posture on cases involving the rights of defendants. In his *Miranda* dissent, he rejected what he thought was the Court's effort to bar from evidence any admission obtained from a suspect, involuntary or not. Like Harlan and Clark, White disagreed with the majority's deep-seated distrust of all confessions and of the efforts by law enforcement officers to obtain such incriminating statements. The essence of White's dissent declares that the majority opinion, despite the chief justice's claim, was without historical foundation:

> *The proposition that the privilege against self-incrimination forbids in-custody interrogation without the warnings specified in the majority opinion and without a clear waiver of counsel has no significant support in the history of the privilege or in the language of the Fifth Amendment. As for the English authorities and the common-law history, the privilege, firmly established in the second half of the seventeenth century, was never applied except to prohibit compelled judicial interrogations. The rule excluding coerced confessions matured about 100 years later, "[b]ut there is nothing in the reports to suggest that the theory has its roots in the privilege against self-incrimination. And so far as the cases reveal, the privilege, as such, seems to have been given effect only in judicial proceedings, including the preliminary examinations by authorized magistrates."[21]*

The release of the *Miranda* decision occurred on the closing day of the Court's 1965–66 term. Despite the obvious tension, the justices left the Court in a relaxed mood to enjoy their traditional end-of-the-term picnic in Montrose Park in Georgetown.

WHAT DID THE DECISION MEAN?

For Ernest Miranda the decision did not mean immediate freedom. Like Clarence Gideon, he would be permitted a new trial. This time, however, the prosecutors would not be able to use his confession. Beyond this narrow and personalized significance, the decision had a far-reaching impact for law enforcement officers. They would now have to follow the Court's specific requirements:

First, a suspect in police custody must be advised prior to questioning that he or she has a right to remain silent and that anything he or she says can be used as evidence against him or her.

Second, a suspect has a right to have counsel present during questioning and to free counsel if he or she cannot afford to retain counsel. A suspect must be notified of these rights prior to questioning.

Third, an interrogation cannot begin unless the suspect makes a voluntary, knowing, and intelligent waiver of the rights just described. The prosecution has a heavy burden of proof in establishing that such a waiver occurred.

Fourth, if a suspect indicates, in any way at anytime, that he or she does not want to be questioned, then questioning must cease. Likewise, if a suspect indicates that he or she wants to consult with counsel, questioning must cease immediately and not resume until counsel is present.

Fifth, violation of any of the foregoing rules automatically bars the admission of a suspect's statements against him or her at trial.

Sixth, the fact that a suspect remained silent or refused to answer questions may not be used by the prosecution at trial.[22]

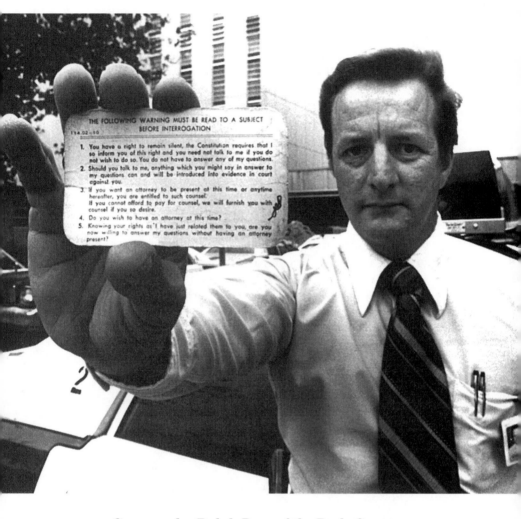

THE FOLLOWING WARNING MUST BE READ TO A SUBJECT
BEFORE INTERROGATION

114.02—10

1. You have a right to remain silent, the Constitution requires that I so inform you of this right and you need not talk to me if you do not wish to do so. You do not have to answer any of my questions.

2. Should you talk to me, anything which you might say in answer to my questions can and will be introduced into evidence in court against you.

3. If you want an attorney to be present at this time or anytime hereafter, you are entitled to such counsel. If you cannot afford to pay for counsel, we will furnish you with counsel if you so desire.

4. Do you wish to have an attorney at this time?

5. Knowing your rights as I have just related them to you, are you now willing to answer my questions without having an attorney present?

Commander Ralph Page of the Dade County (Florida) Public Safety Department shows a Miranda *card, which spells out the police procedures required by the Supreme Court in* Miranda. *Police officers throughout the United States continue to use these cards to warn suspects of their right to remain silent and their right to counsel.*

These requirements were to apply to all defendants without regard to age, education, intelligence, or prior experience with the law. As with its ruling in *Gideon*, the Court wanted to create a specific requirement not dependent upon the unique characteristics of the suspect. Police and law enforcement officials must treat all defendants equally from the time of arrest.

In his article, "Reconsidering Miranda," law professor Stephen Schulhofer helped clarify the essence of the Court's decision. He found, first, that compulsion, within the meaning of the Fifth Amendment, can include informal pressure to speak. Second, he related that any custodial interrogation involves enough pressure to constitute "compulsion" within the meaning of the Fifth Amendment. And, third, he noted the necessity for using the codelike rules that warn the defendant of his or her rights.[23]

Any Supreme Court decision will have both broad and narrow implications. In the next chapter we will examine what this landmark case meant for Ernest Miranda in his retrial as well as for police and prosecutors across the nation.

Chapter 6
THE IMPACT OF *MIRANDA*

Every Supreme Court decision has both a very narrow, personalized, and immediate impact on the individuals involved and a broader, more theoretical, and long-range impact on future Supreme Court cases. It is hard to imagine any decision creating a greater distance between the personal impact and the public impact than the decision in *Miranda v. Arizona*. Let's look at the shocking contrast between what the Supreme Court's decision meant to Ernest Miranda and its implications for the nation's criminal justice and legal system.

THE RETRIAL AND TRAGIC LIFE OF ERNEST MIRANDA

Upon hearing the wonderful news of his successful appeal to the U.S. Supreme Court, Ernest Miranda became notorious not only within the Arizona State Prison but across the entire nation. Ernest's father,

*Ernest Miranda (right) and attorney
John Flynn (left) discuss defense strategy
during Miranda's 1967 retrial on the
charges of kidnapping and rape.*

like Ernest himself, thought that the Court's decision would result in his son's immediate release from prison, and he rushed out to a liquor store to begin stocking up for a homecoming celebration. Unfortunately for the Miranda family, the plans for a joyous reunion were premature. They failed to realize that the Supreme Court's decision simply offered

Ernest a new trial, and this time the confession that Detectives Cooley and Young had extracted from him would not be admitted as evidence.

Although Miranda achieved celebrity status among his fellow inmates for his Supreme Court victory, he had to wait eight months for his retrial. It was originally scheduled for October 24, 1966, but the victim and most critical witness, Lois Ann Jameson, was expecting a baby in November, and the Court postponed the new trial until mid-February. John Flynn, the attorney who won his appeal, continued to represent Miranda, but for the retrial the prosecution upgraded the quality of its representation. Maricopa County's chief prosecutor, Robert Corbin, took charge of the case. The greater significance attached to Miranda's retrial became apparent when highly respected Superior Court Judge Lawrence K. Wren was imported from Flagstaff to preside over the case. All of these changes reflected the national attention focused on Miranda's trial; a case that three-and-one-half years earlier had simply been another violent crime in a working-class suburb of Phoenix that failed to attract even local interest.

As the February trial date drew near, Miranda and his attorney grew increasingly optimistic. At one point Flynn approached the prosecutor and inquired why he even bothered trying to reconvict his client, and Corbin candidly answered that he realized he didn't have much of a chance but "at least I'll go down fighting."[1]

Corbin, however, received an unexpected break. Miranda's former common-law wife, Twila Hoffman, had approached him seeking help. She feared that if Miranda obtained his freedom, he might hurt her or her young child, which she had conceived by another man while Miranda was in prison. In conversations with Corbin, Hoffman disclosed that on a visit to Miranda in jail while he was awaiting his original trial, Ernest had confessed to her that he had kidnapped and raped Jameson. To confirm her story, Corbin sent Detective Carroll Cooley to interview Hoffman again. She repeated the jail confession to Cooley and elaborated further, stating that Miranda had told her "to get in touch with Lois Ann [Jameson] and give her his promise to marry her if she would agree to drop charges against him—he would return to Mrs. Hoffman later."[2]

With these new developments, Chief Prosecutor Corbin began to feel optimistic about his chances during the retrial, scheduled to begin on Wednesday, February 15, 1967. The entire case seemed to hinge on the question of whether the judge would allow the jury to hear Twila Hoffman's testimony about Miranda's jailhouse confession. The trial lasted nine days, but only about eight hours were spent in open court before the jury. The rest of the time was devoted to arguments, usually in the judge's chambers, between Flynn and Corbin over which evidence should be admitted or suppressed. After days of meticulous research, Judge Wren decided to admit Hoffman's incriminating testimony. The jury deliberated for only eighty-three minutes before finding Ernest Miranda guilty of kidnapping and rape. Two weeks later the judge sentenced him to twenty to thirty years in the Arizona State Prison. It was exactly one year after the U.S. Supreme Court had overturned Miranda's original conviction; his father's planned celebration would never occur.

Miranda returned to prison, his brief period of freedom following the 1966 Supreme Court decision was a distant blur in his memory. Although he be-

Robert Corbin, Maricopa County's chief prosecutor, could not use the station house confession in Miranda's retrial. He did, however, convince the trial judge to admit a later jailhouse confession by Miranda as evidence. The jury found Miranda guilty of kidnapping and rape.

came eligible for parole in 1970, the State Parole Board rejected Miranda's first four requests until it finally granted his release in December 1972. Miranda returned to the home of his stepmother and two brothers in Mesa in time for Christmas, but it was rather subdued since his father had died in an automobile accident only two months earlier. Miranda appeared anxious to try and straighten out his life. He had written a friend from prison the previous year: "You must know how bad I want to obtain my release. But not just a release. I want to make something of myself, to obtain an education and elevate myself in society. I know that this will be hard for me but, only at first."[3]

Miranda had been sincere in his efforts to improve himself as he worked during his last two years in prison to earn his high school equivalency degree. He also learned how to be a skilled barber, cutting the hair of both guards and inmates in return for cigarettes. Unfortunately, Arizona law prohibited ex-felons from obtaining a barber's license, and he was forced to settle for another series of menial jobs similar to those he held prior to entering prison: warehouseman, produce man, and delivery truck driver. They barely paid minimum wage. Miranda remained extremely unhappy and frustrated during this entire time. He felt he had somehow been cheated out of the expected rewards that were to flow from his 1966 Supreme Court victory. His name may have had celebrity status in the hallways of law schools and courthouses, but his actual life had been mired in misery and disappointment.

Miranda continued to have trouble avoiding problems with the police. He was continually stopped for a variety of traffic violations, the result of both his local fame and his erratic style of driving.

On Sunday, July 23, 1974, the Tempe, Arizona, police stopped him for driving on the wrong side of the road. The police officer quickly discovered that Miranda had no license or any other form of identification other than a yellowed newspaper clipping about his 1966 Supreme Court victory. A further search of the car uncovered a loaded revolver hidden under the driver's seat. When the officer frisked him, he found three amphetamines. Miranda was transported to the county jail and charged with the possession of a firearm and possession of illicit drugs.

Miranda was able to obtain the services of a well-respected local criminal lawyer, Henry J. Florence, who convinced the trial judge that the police officer's search of the car had been unconstitutional because it had failed to satisy the probable cause standard. This standard requires police to have a reasonable suspicion that a crime has been committed before they search a suspect. The judge dropped the charges, but the possession of a gun and drugs violated Miranda's conditions of parole, and he was returned in January 1975 to Arizona State Prison in Florence to serve the remainder of his original sentence on the kidnapping and rape conviction. He was now thirty-three years old and had spent nine of his last thirteen years in the inhospitable confines of the Florence prison.

He served approximately one more year in prison before being released in late fall 1975. His brief flirtation with life outside of the prison walls ended tragically. Miranda had been living in a Phoenix flophouse, working again as a delivery man for an appliance store. The police thought he had begun dealing drugs but had no hard evidence. On Saturday night, January 31, 1976, Miranda went to a neighborhood bar, La Amapala, to relax and play

Fernando Zamora Rodriguez was arrested in connection with the January 1976 murder of Ernest Miranda. A little more than three years after receiving a pardon, Miranda was stabbed to death following a barroom brawl.

some cards. He entered into a poker game with two illegal Mexican immigrants. All three had been drinking. Soon charges of cheating led to a loud argument and a violent fist fight. After the dust cleared, Miranda went to the men's room to wash his bloody hands. When Miranda returned, one of the men drew a knife and stabbed him twice, once in the stomach and also in the upper chest. He was dead before the emergency crew could reach the hospital. The killer disappeared into the night, although his accomplice was caught and, ironically, read his rights from the *Miranda* warning card carried by all Phoenix police. The brief, dramatic life of Ernest Miranda was over. Only his legacy as a name attached to a landmark constitutional law decision would survive.

Let's now move from the depressing personal side of this case to its broader consequences as it affected police, prosecution, and judicial behavior across the country, reaching even the most distant police stations and criminal courthouses.

THE ISSUE OF RETROACTIVITY

Ernest Miranda was not the only inmate sitting in a state prison who had confessed to a crime without the advice of counsel and within the intimidating atmosphere of a police station. Thousands of other prisoners anxiously awaited the result of the *Miranda* decision. Once it was handed down, they too hoped their confessions would be ruled inadmissible and be granted a retrial. The U.S. Supreme Court, and especially its chief justice, understood the practical ramifications of the retroactivity question in the *Miranda* decision. Thus, there was little surprise when the Court confronted this problem directly in the case of *Johnson v. New Jersey* (1966), decided only one week after *Miranda*. The Court concluded first that its *Escobedo* decision—which required that detainees be advised of their right to counsel once they had become the focus of an investigation and the purpose of the police interrogation was to obtain a confession—affected only those cases in which the trial began after June 22, 1964 (the date of that decision). Secondly, the Court ruled: "We hold further that *Miranda* applies only to cases in which the trial began after the date of that decision one week ago [June 13, 1966]."[4] The decision in *Johnson* was consistent with other recent Supreme Court rulings that denied the retroactive effect to *Mapp v. Ohio* (a 1961 case involving the inadmissibility of illegally obtained evidence in state criminal proceedings) and *Griffin v. California* (a 1965 case involving the prohibition against prosecutors and judges commenting on the failure of a defendant to take the stand).

Warren was already beginning to hear a growing wail of congressional and judicial criticism. With only Justices Black and Douglas dissenting, the chief justice wrote that "retroactive application of *Escobedo* and *Miranda* would seriously disrupt the administration of our criminal laws. It would require the retrial or release of numerous prisoners found guilty by trustworthy evidence in conformity with previously announced constitutional standards."[5] As we shall now see, despite Warren's hopes that the *Johnson* decision would help to minimize the expected public outcry against *Miranda*, the national reaction was unprecedented.

PUBLIC, PROFESSIONAL, AND POLITICAL REACTION TO *MIRANDA*

The public generally has either no reaction or a somewhat benign reaction to most Supreme Court decisions. The Court's pronouncements rarely are covered on the evening television news or make newspaper headlines. Occasionally a decision such as *Brown v. Board of Education of Topeka* (1954) or *Gideon v. Wainwright* (1963) will gain national attention and receive a positive public response. During the 1960s, however, the Warren Court began making decisions that were increasingly upsetting to the public. The *Miranda* decision marked a high point in the public outcry and media publicity concerning a Warren Court decision. An emotional response was heard not only from politicians and the legal community but also from angry citizens.

Part of the explanation for this vocal negative reaction may have been the historical context in which the decision was delivered. The spring of 1966 was not a peaceful time in our nation's history. The escalation of the war in Vietnam and its resulting carnage was beginning to drive a wedge between many Americans. The nation was also beginning to experience the first in a series of urban disturbances. These outbreaks of violence would unleash an emotional backlash that seemed to make "crime in the streets" the nation's number one domestic issue. When the Court handed down its decisions in *Miranda* and *Johnson*, it had been less than a year since the first rioting broke out in the Watts section of Los Angeles in August 1965, leaving thirty-seven dead, thousands injured, and hundreds of stores and homes burned to the ground. Lawlessness was a concern of nearly every middle-class American. Who was to blame? Who was to protect us?

Many Americans had traditionally depended upon the police to arrest law breakers and upon judges and courts to sentence them to prison. The *Miranda* decision was handed down just as the public was being told of rising crime rates and increasing violence. Could the police be depended upon to protect a fearful public, one that was afraid to walk out into the threatening streets? Both politicians and police, possibly hoping to deflect blame for their own ineffectiveness in dealing with urban crime, began to point toward the judiciary as the possible culprit for this escalating violence. Not only were state and local judges too lenient in their sentencing practices, the argument went, now with decisions such as *Escobedo* and *Miranda*, the highest court in the land had handcuffed the police by undermining their capacity to extract confessions from defendants they had arrested. Public safety appeared to be sacrificed for defendant's rights. These unworthy individuals would be given free attorneys as soon as they were taken into custody, and they could no longer be interrogated if they and their attorneys decided it was not in their best interests.

Politicians in Washington and in state legislatures across the country responded to the public's concern and quickly drafted many bills designed to minimize or even eradicate the impact of the *Miranda* decision. Although most of the legislative efforts were not successful, they stirred much debate and permitted many politicians to voice concern over the situation. Senator Sam Ervin's comments in 1966 in support of one such federal bill is typical of the reaction. He accused the Supreme Court of showing "excessive and visional solicitude for the accused by inventing new rules to turn loose on society self-confessed criminals."[6]

Congress held hearings on developing legislation designed to limit *Miranda*'s impact. Although the legislation would only apply to federal crimes and crimes in the District of Columbia, and thereby not affect state and local law enforcement, it was hoped it would spark a series of similar bills in numerous state legislatures. The anti-*Miranda* bill was included within Title II of the Omnibus Crime Control and Safe Street Acts, a broad criminal law reform package. After much debate, the Senate drafted a revised voluntariness standard for the admission of confessions in federal prosecutions into section 3501 of the new act. This section was harshly criticized by liberal Democrats as well as the Johnson Administration, but it remained intact as the larger Omnibus Crime Bill became law in 1968. Because of its narrow applicability, as well as the hostility it faced within the Johnson Administration, Section 3501 failed to have a meaningful impact on federal prosecutions or to spark similar laws at the state level.

Police officials, as one might expect, were very upset over the *Miranda* decision. Their nearly uniform reaction was to criticize the Supreme Court for what they believed was an unwarranted criticism of their interrogation practices. Typical statements from police chiefs around the nation included the following:

- In Boston, Police Commissioner Edmund L. McNamara complained that "criminal trials no longer will be a search for the truth but a search for technical error."
- In Cleveland, Chief of Police Richard Wagner, disagreeing with the Supreme Court's belief that *Miranda* would not eliminate future confessions, complained that "there is no such thing as a voluntary statement. While the Supreme Court Justices say there is, they have made it impossible to obtain one."
- In Philadelphia, Police Commissioner Edward J. Bell declared that "the present rules and interpretation whether or not so intended, in fact protect the guilty. I do not believe

the Constitution was designed as a shield for criminals."[7]

The reaction from lower federal courts and state courts was not nearly as uniform or as bitter as the criticism that came from the general public and law enforcement officials. Most of the judges from the federal system, especially those from the various circuit courts of appeal, were supportive of the *Miranda* decision. The majority of the criticism seemed to arise from the sharply divided opinion of state appellate and trial judges who would be the first line of judicial officers forced to implement *Miranda* in their courts. Representative of the responses of federal appellate judges, Judge Walter L. Pope of the U.S. Circuit Court of Appeals for the Ninth Circuit stated in an address at the Ninth Circuit's annual judicial conference in 1966: "It seems plain that in *Escobedo* and in *Miranda* the Court majority was again intervening in the governing process to deal with and correct practices which it found, as commonly employed by police, operated to infringe upon the constitutional privilege against self-incrimination through in-custody interrogation. . . . We shall be able to live with this decision." In a lighter vein, he added that "those most affected by the decision were not police or the general public but the authors of police manuals such as professors Inbau and Reid who may never be able to sell their books again."[8]

Many of the leading state jurists were critical of the *Miranda* decision and sounded remarkably like the police and prosecutors. Judge Edward S. Piggins from Michigan's Third Judicial Circuit captured this sentiment with his reaction. He felt in agreement "with an American public that voices a vigorous protest when it watches confessed rapists and murderers go free to repeat their crimes because their confessions have been barred from evidence for what appears to the lay public, at least, to be an unrelated technicality."[9]

SUBSEQUENT SUPREME COURT DECISIONS AFFECTING *MIRANDA*

Although the reactions of both federal and state judges throughout the country was an important indicator of the legal profession's attitude toward the *Miranda* decision, it was not as significant as the Supreme Court's subsequent decisions regarding the admissibility of confessions. Because the United States is a common law country, its changing judicial policies are developed not through legal codes, such as one finds in Germany or France, but rather through its subsequent Supreme Court decisions. Despite the clamor of legislators to undermine the impact of *Miranda* through legislation, the only viable means to rectify or modify the Court's decisions controlling the admissibility of confessions is through future Supreme Court decisions and their interpretation of this complex and emotional issue. In tracing the voluminous number of forthcoming cases affecting the *Miranda* decision, it becomes clear why *Miranda* was probably the most important Warren Court decision affecting the rights of persons accused of crimes.

The remainder of this chapter will review the most important Supreme Court decisions in the thirty years since *Miranda* was decided. These cases fall into two broad categories:

1. Decisions that attempted to clarify *Miranda* by touching on the many corollary issues growing out of the decision. Examples of this category of subsequent Supreme Court decisions are: cases dealing with the voluntary

confession of mentally ill or deficient defendants; application of *Miranda* to grand jury
testimony; what constitutes a satisfactory
waiver of the Fifth Amendment's protection
against self-incrimination; and whether
questionable confessions may be used for impeachment purposes during the trial.
2. Decisions that were designed to weaken the
impact of the original decision. Although *Miranda* has never been directly overruled and
is still a valid precedent today, many of the
post-1966 Supreme Court decisions have attempted to undermine its ability to limit police interrogations. Examples of issues
decided within this general category are: the
development of the harmless error rule and
the public safety exception; restrictions on
the definition and parameters of custodial interrogation; and the role of informants in
eliciting confessions.

Let's first examine a varied array of cases that attempted to clarify rather than undermine the
Miranda decision. Because of the importance of the
defendant's state of mind during a station house
interrogation, a difficult issue arises when a confession is made by a defendant who suffers from mental illness. How voluntary is such a confession?
Miranda himself was of questionable emotional
stability as well as marginal intelligence. The
Supreme Court attempted to resolve this complex
question in *Colorado v. Connelly* (1986). The case
arose out of the August 1983 arrest of Frances Connelly in Denver, Colorado. Connelly had walked over
to police officer Patrick Anderson and told him that
he murdered someone and wanted to talk about it.

The police officer read him his rights, which Connelly said he understood and insisted on talking anyway. He also informed the policeman that he had been institutionalized in five different mental institutions. Connelly told a homicide detective that he had returned from Boston to confess that he had murdered a young girl, Mary Ann Junta, in November 1982. He took the police to the scene of the crime, and police recovered Junta's body. During this time, the police did not notice that Connelly was suffering from a mental illness.

The next day Connelly spoke with a public defender, who found him visibly disoriented and claiming that he was hearing voices. At this point local authorities sent him to a state psychiatric hospital, where he was evaluated and found to be incompetent to assist in his own defense. By March 1984, however, doctors thought Connelly was competent to go to trial, and he subsequently was convicted of murder. By a 7–2 vote, the U.S. Supreme Court held that Connelly's confession was voluntary because the police had complied with *Miranda,* although the defendant, at the time he confessed, was hearing voices telling him to confess. The majority also held that the state is required to prove there was a *Miranda* waiver only by a preponderance of the evidence and that a defendant's waiver will be considered involuntary under the Fifth Amendment only if police coercion is involved. The essence of the Court's opinion was that:

> *The sole concern of the Fifth Amendment, upon which* Miranda *was based, is governmental coercion; Fifth Amendment privilege is not concerned with moral and psychological pressures to confess emanating from*

*sources other than official coercion.Voluntari-
ness of waiver of right to remain silent depends upon absence of police overreaching,
not on "free choice" in any broader sense of the
word.*[10]

The complex issue of when has a defendant satis-
factorily "waived" his or her Fifth Amendment protections has generated much discussion and many
Supreme Court rulings. In *Michigan v. Mosley*
(1975) the Court, by a 6–2 vote, was willing to allow
a defendant to waive this right even after he initially chose to remain silent. Thus, under the rules
established in *Mosley*, police questioning may be resumed at least in the following circumstances:

1. the original interrogation is promptly termi-
   nated
2. the questioning is resumed only after the
   passage of a significant period of time
3. the suspect is given a fresh set of warnings at
   the second session
4. a different officer resumes the questioning
5. the second interrogation is restricted to a
   crime that had not been the subject of the
   earlier interrogation
6. the second interrogation occurs at another location.

According to a leading constitutional law scholar,
Yale Kamisar of the University of Michigan Law
School, the first three circumstances appear to be
minimal requirements for the resumption of questioning once a person asserts his or her right to remain silent. Kamisar agrees with the dissenters in
Mosley, who charge that *Mosley* fails to clarify exactly when the police can resume questioning:

Although in Mosley *the Court made clear that the requirement that the police "scrupulously honor" the suspect's assertion of his right to remain silent is independent of the requirement that any waiver be knowing, intelligent, and voluntary—thus rejecting the most restricted interpretation of* Miranda *in this respect (an interpretation advanced by Justice White)—it would have done better to adopt the position advocated by the dissenters. They argued that either arraignment or counsel must be provided before resumption of questioning of one who has previously invoked the privilege. "Instead, [the Court] in* Mosley *chose to chart a middle course which offers only ambiguous protection to the accused and virtually no guidance to the police or the courts who must live with the rule.*[11]

Another area left unclear by *Miranda* was how a defendant's earlier statements may be used not just as a confession to the crime but to impeach the defendant's credibility if he or she takes the stand. This issue came up only five years after *Miranda* in the case of *Harris v. New York* (1971). Despite strong dissents by justices Brennan, Marshall, and Douglas, the Court held in *Harris* that statements preceded by defective *Miranda* warnings, and thus inadmissible for the prosecution's case, could be used by prosecutors to attack the credibility of the defendant's testimony if he or she decided to take the stand in his or her own defense. Law professor Jerrold Israel believes that the *Harris* decision was even more important for prosecutors than for police:

A major value in obtaining a statement from a defendant, even where the defendant does

*not acknowledge commission of the offense,
is the discovery provided regarding the
defendant's likely trial testimony. While the
defendant may shift somewhat from the explanation in his statement, the statement's
availability for impeachment should keep the
defendant's testimony close to that original
explanation. Of course, if the statement is incriminating, then the* Harris *ruling is likely to
have even more value from the prosecution's
viewpoint. It may place the defendant in a position where he will be forced to take the
chance involved in not testifying at all. If he
takes the stand, the statement surely will be
damaging notwithstanding the judge's admonition to the jury that they can consider the
incriminating admissions only as to impeachment and not as substantive evidence.*[12]

Another Supreme Court decision, *Oregon v. Hass*
(1975), carried the impeachment issue even further.
In this instance the defendant had been advised of
his rights and asserted them. Nevertheless, the police refused to honor the suspect's request for a
lawyer and continued to question him. The Court
held that the prosecution was permitted to use this
additional information for impeachment purposes
despite the troublesome nature of the circumstances.

The second category of post-*Miranda* decisions
were more pointedly intended to weaken the impact
of *Miranda* and permit police and prosecutors an opportunity to interrogate prisoners effectively. The
impeachment cases of *Harris* and *Hass* could also
have been placed within this second category, but we
will begin our discussion with *Michigan v. Tucker*

(1974). In *Tucker* Justice William Rehnquist dealt with the issue of the application of the "fruit of the poisonous tree doctrine" to the testimony of a witness uncovered as a result of a police interrogation that had violated the *Miranda* requirements, but had occurred before *Miranda* was decided. (Under the "fruit of the poisonous tree doctrine," evidence that has been seized illegally is considered tainted and cannot be used against a suspect.) The Court held that, in light of the special problems raised by attempting to apply *Miranda* to pre-*Miranda* interrogations, it was inappropriate to expand the impact by excluding the witness's testimony as well as the defendant's statement. Rehnquist, however, went even further, suggesting in his majority opinion that the Court in the future might not extend the "poisoned fruits doctrine" to the tainted witness even where retroactive application is not involved.

The Court later issued a pair of decisions designed to clarify and limit the area defined to be a coercive environment of custodial interrogation. In *Mathiason v. Oregon* (1977) the Supreme Court decided that because Mathiason had not been placed in true custody—he had not been under arrest and was free to leave—*Miranda* did not apply. The Court held that "any interview of one suspected of a crime by a police officer will have coercive aspects to it simply by virtue of the fact that the police officer is part of a law enforcement system which may ultimately cause the suspect to be charged with a crime. But police officers are not required to administer *Miranda* warnings to everyone whom they question. Nor is the requirement of warnings to be imposed simply because the questioning takes place in a station house. . . . *Miranda* warnings are required only where there has been such a restric-

Justice Rehnquist delivered the Supreme Court's opinion in Michigan v. Tucker *(1974). The Court ruled that the testimony of a witness, whose identity had been discovered during a police interrogation in which the suspect had not been informed of his* Miranda *rights, could be used as evidence.*

tion on a person's freedom as to render him 'in custody.'"[13] In a closely related case, *Beckwith v. U.S.* (1976), the Court ruled that a defendant questioned by I.R.S. agents in his home had not been placed in the type of custodial interrogation situation envisioned by the Court in *Miranda.* Thus, unless a suspect is actually subjected to the coercive pressures generated in a police station–like atmosphere and there are apparent restraints present, *Miranda* is not applicable.

Many analysts believe *New York v. Quarles* (1985) is the one case that has most undermined the spirit of the *Miranda* decision. In *Quarles*, police apprehended a suspect in a supermarket, handcuffed him, and noticed that his gun holster was empty. They questioned the suspect about the location of the gun before reading him his *Miranda* rights. The Court ruled that when a police officer's questions are necessary to protect his safety, his fellow officers, or the public, the answers are admissible as evidence even though the defendant is in custody and no warning has been given. *Quarles* cut out a major exception to the *Miranda* holding, and it represents the most direct threat to both the legal rationale and the practical accomplishment of *Miranda.* Critics of the decision believe that the primary danger posed by *Quarles* is in its practical applications. Attorney Robert Jacobs points out that "if one form of compelled statement is admissible when elicited in the interest of public safety then surely others are too— if the prosecution can demonstrate that the public danger is great. Even absent actual physical coercion, we may now see a return to litigation over the kinds of psychological and fear inducing tricks that were part of the standard police interrogation before *Miranda.*"[14]

Five years after *Quarles*, the Supreme Court handed down another decision that chipped away at the beleaguered *Miranda* decision. In *Illinois v. Perkins* (1990), a seven-justice majority held that an undercover law enforcement officer posing as a fellow inmate need not give *Miranda* warnings to an incarcerated suspect before asking questions that may elicit an incriminating response. Justice Anthony Kennedy, who authored the majority opinion, explained that where an incarcerated suspect is simply fooled, law enforcement domination of the environment is linked with constitutionally acceptable deception and not with unacceptable coercion. Not everyone agrees with Justice Kennedy's explanation, but overall *Perkins* has not created a major exception to *Miranda*. What it has done, according to criminal justice professor Fred Cohen, is to join:

> *a long list of decisions giving constitutional validity to various forms of official fraud and deceit and to the growing use of informers. Virtually all prisons and jails now use an informer network to obtain information and maintain security.* Perkins *is a criminal procedure decision that will give further encouragement to such systems and thereby add another chill to already limited speech and another measure of distrust for one's keepers and colleagues. At the station house, we may expect more elaborate hoaxes especially in the "big cases."*[15]

Finally, in *Arizona v. Fulminante* (1991) the Supreme Court overturned earlier case law and held that a conviction can stand even if the confession admitted as evidence in the case is involuntary or coerced as long as the confession is deemed "harmless." Under this ruling a confession is deemed harmless when the state can demonstrate that the admission of the confession did not contribute to the conviction. The Court held that the confession in *Fulminante* was coerced and *harmful* and, therefore, inadmissible. The Court, however, went on to make a ruling applicable to other instances in which the error was harmless. Before one can grasp the significance of the *Fulminante* decision and its "harmless era" doctrine, one will have to wait for future cases to reach the court and hopefully clarify what is presently open to wide conjecture.

A CONCLUDING COMMENT

Following the resignation of Chief Justice Earl Warren and the election of President Richard Nixon, many judicial scholars who had applauded the *Miranda* decision as a hallmark in the protection of defendants accused of crime feared that the decision would soon be overturned. These fears grew as conservative presidents Ronald Reagan and George Bush were elected and had several opportunities to nominate members to the Supreme Court. Detractors of the *Miranda* decision, primarily from the political right, optimistically hoped that new Court members would soon directly overrule *Miranda*, a decision that symbolized all that was disliked about the Warren Court. Our cursory review of the impact of this landmark decision has shown that in the three decades since *Miranda* was decided, the predictions of both groups have gone unfulfilled. Yes, the Court has undermined and weakened the original *Miranda* ruling through such decisions as *Quarles*, *Perkins*, *Harris*, and *Mosley*, but none of these cases amounted to a direct overruling. They have merely nibbled around the edges. The essential holding of *Miranda*, requiring police officers once they arrest a defendant to warn him or her of the right to remain silent and the right to counsel has continued unshaken.

Chapter 7

THE LEGACY OF MIRANDA FOR THE 21ST CENTURY

This concluding chapter will focus on three primary topics. First we will explore the basic question of exactly what the impact of the *Miranda* decision has been upon the effectiveness of police and law enforcement officers in their difficult battle against crime. Has the *Miranda* requirement that the police warn criminals about their constitutional rights, especially their right to remain silent, significantly handicapped law enforcement officers during the interrogation process to the degree that critics of the decision claim? We'll then turn to broader issues related to the impact of *Miranda v. Arizona* decision, such as federalism and the concept of separation of powers. The final area of investigation will be an effort to place the *Miranda* decision in its proper historical perspective. Was the case the pinnacle of the Warren Court's due process revolution, and what is the position of the present Court on the issues raised in *Miranda*?

HANDCUFFING THE POLICE: A REVIEW OF POLICE BEHAVIOR AFTER *MIRANDA*

It is difficult to measure the magnitude of *Miranda*'s impact upon police effectiveness. There have been many studies conducted by both legal scholars and social scientists that have attempted to answer this question. Typically the studies have focused upon a specific locale and have examined police behavior for a period of time, often comparing their pre- and post-*Miranda* performance. The overall conclusion of these varied studies is that the *Miranda* decision did not exert the feared decrease in police effectiveness. A minority of studies did imply that in certain categories of crimes the police would be marginally less effective, but even these studies failed to substantiate the claims of *Miranda* detractors that police performance would be significantly undermined by the Supreme Court's stringent requirements.

The first study, and the one most frequently cited, was conducted in New Haven, Connecticut, by the student members of the Yale Law School *Law Review*. They tested the proposition that defendants would be less likely to make confessions following the *Miranda* decision because they would have been warned or advised of their rights. The study refuted the premise, finding that confession rates remained the same. One explanation for this steady state is that there is a good deal of psychological pressure on suspects to respond to police questioning, even if they have been informed of their rights.

The Yale study was conducted in the summer of 1966. Observing police interrogations around the clock for eleven weeks, the law students were able to witness 127 interrogations of ninety defendants. They also interviewed twenty-one New Haven detectives and fifty-five local defense attorneys. The study not only analyzed the impact of *Miranda* on a suspect's willingness to talk with police, but it also examined the decision's effect upon police officer morale. The study concluded that warnings seldom prompted defendants either to refuse to answer questions or to request counsel. It appeared that substantial pressure to confess continued.

The Yale study also concluded that police interrogation might not be as crucial to criminal investigation as many *Miranda* critics had alleged. The report estimated it was necessary in only 13 percent of the observed cases, although the detectives themselves placed the figure at 21 percent.[1] Turning to the issue of *Miranda*'s effect upon police morale, the Yale–New Haven study disclosed that the detectives viewed the decision as a "slap at policemen everywhere . . . and as a personal rebuke by a Court, that, in their eyes, [knew] very little about police and their problems. These feelings of resentment were intensified by the basic distrust of courts and lawyers, who just made more difficult an already thankless job."[2] Despite these negative sentiments by police officers, the major conclusion of the study was that *Miranda* had a very small impact on law enforcement in New Haven. The study gave two reasons for this result: interrogations played a very minor role in solving crimes in the city, and the rules seemed to exert little effect upon interrogations. The *Miranda* rules did little to reduce the "inherently coercive atmosphere" of police stations, and they were often given in a begrudging fashion designed toward encouraging the suspect to disregard their implications.[3]

A second study, also conducted by a law school, reached similar conclusions. In Washington, D.C., the Institute of Criminal Law and Procedure at the Georgetown University Law Center conducted a

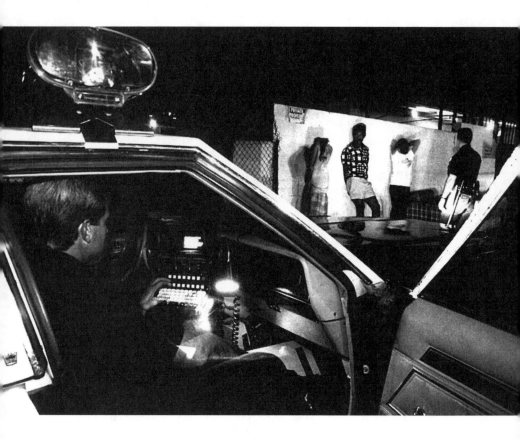

*A Los Angeles Police Department officer uses a
computer to check for outstanding warrants on
three people caught loitering in a back alley.
Several studies have indicated that the* Miranda
*decision did not result in the harm to police effec-
tiveness that the decision's detractors had feared.*

study of the Precinct Representation Project, a
large-scale effort to provide volunteer attorneys to
suspects on a twenty-four-hour basis, seven days a
week. A team of researchers observed the program

for a year. Using detailed reports, team observations, and numerous interviews, the authors found "that an astonishingly small number of suspects availed themselves of the free legal assistance provided by the project. (The exact figure was seven percent of felony or serious misdemeanor suspects.)"[4]

The Georgetown study closed with a critical statement that the premises underlying the *Miranda* decision were questionable, specifically the belief that the police would give adequate and effective warning of legal rights and that a suspect would understand the significance of the warnings and be able to make an intelligent choice about waiving his or her right to remain silent or request counsel.[5] The report's comment based on interviews with volunteer attorneys was equally disturbing: interrogation was required by so few arrests that the lawyers felt they were wasting their time waiting at the station house.[6]

A third research effort was conducted in Denver a few years later, and it reached findings consistent with the earlier studies in New Haven and Washington, D.C. A few interesting variations, however, did appear. The study concentrated on the perceptions of the suspects. By the time of this study, the summer of 1969, the Denver police were regularly advising suspects of their rights—a practice not so uniformly performed in the earlier studies. Researchers interviewed fifty suspects who had been interrogated by police, and the suspects disclosed that there had been a high degree of compliance with the *Miranda* requirements, although upon closer examination, there were serious gaps in comprehension. Examples of confusion among the suspects is indicated by the finding that 60 percent of the suspects thought that under no circumstances could their signing a waiver have any legal effect and 45 percent believed that oral statements could not be used against them. This study, therefore, creates doubt as to how intelligent were the waiver decisions being made by these defendants.[7]

The three studies just reviewed are fairly representative of the many investigations into the impact of the *Miranda* decision upon police behavior. Taken as a whole they seem to offer two major findings: (1) The new rules have only slightly lowered the number of confessions, and because confessions at the station house were a relatively rare occurrence even in the pre-*Miranda* years, the decision has done little to seriously affect overall police effectiveness; and (2) The decision has had a perceptible impact on the morale of police officers and in many instances resulted in fairly widespread noncompliance.

In 1966, and in the following five to ten years, the police came under serious criticism for being unable to control the escalating crime rates, especially in urban areas. They had become scapegoats for the public's growing frustration and fear. Someone had to be blamed, and the police and courts were the most likely targets. The police response to these generally unwarranted accusations was to then turn toward the judiciary, and especially the Supreme Court, and blame the courts for the seeming inability of police departments to protect society. Decisions such as *Miranda* were characterized as handcuffing the police and undermining their capacity to control the criminal element. The public seemed to accept this explanation and joined the police in their harsh and persistent criticism of the Supreme Court.

Courts have traditionally tried to remove themselves from the political fray and remain silent in the face of public criticism. Unfortunately this failure to respond to criticisms of the *Miranda* decision only seemed to fuel the fires of angry public charges despite the clear-cut evidence to the contrary, as shown in many scientific studies, such as those conducted in New Haven, Denver, and Washington, D.C.

BROADER ISSUES AFFECTING THE *MIRANDA* LEGACY

Miranda represents more than an effort to force police into less coercive behavior during their interrogation of suspects. The decision provides a clear example of the actions that a judicially active Supreme Court will take when it has grown impatient waiting for the responsible public officials to deal with a serious constitutional problem. As chapter 3 indicated, the Supreme Court, through its earlier precedents, had been sending a fairly clear message to state legislators, judges, and local police officials that coercive practices in eliciting confessions would no longer be allowed. The Warren Court had written a series of decisions in the late 1950s and early 1960s, which culminated in 1964 with *Escobedo*, serving notice that police misconduct in the station house would no longer be tolerated. In the eyes of the Warren Court, the police had failed to correct their errant behavior, and state and local officials had refused to take action. Chief Justice Warren, along with justices Black, Douglas, Brennan, and Fortas, felt compelled to address the situation and chose *Miranda* as a vehicle for clarifying acceptable police practices once an arrest had been made. The Court believed that it had neither acted impatiently nor defied earlier precedent in *Miranda* but rather had written a decision that was a logical advancement of the rights of criminal defendants begun earlier during the Warren Court years. Several years after leaving the Court, former Justice Goldberg expressed his views on the fairness of the U.S. legal system:

*Ensuring equal treatment for the rich and
poor and for the federal and state defendant,
rearticulating and redefining previously rec-
ognized rights without moving markedly forward or backward with respect to the expanse
of these rights—none of these aims seems un-
reasonable. The Warren Court concentrated
on strengthening the defenses of the individual's rights—entrenching along boundaries
already set out long ago. In fact, what the
Court was doing can be justified on strict constitutional and stare decisis grounds.*[8]

In addition to being criticized for being impatient,
Warren and his colleagues were faulted for their
willingness to interfere in what was believed by
many to be a local law enforcement problem. It was
the State of Arizona that should decide what
Phoenix police practices should be, not the U.S.
Supreme Court sitting majestically nearly three
thousand miles away. Police conduct, the argument
went, was a local issue and should therefore be han-
dled through state or local means. This attitude was
clearly rejected by the Warren Court, which argued
that its responsibilities in a federal system of government required it to ensure that all defendants
would receive fair and just treatment as required by
the due process clause of the Fourteenth Amendment. Thus, before any defendant risked the loss of
his or her freedom, the Supreme Court had a clear
responsibility to ensure that all relevant protections
of the federal Bill of Rights were bestowed upon all
persons in any jurisdiction. The Court tried to reas-
sure localities that states are free to develop their
own safeguards for the privilege of ensuring that defendants are not being coerced into incriminating
themselves, but the Court did add the caveat that

this freedom was not without limits and could only
be exercised "so long as they are fully effective as
those described above in informing accused persons
of their right of silence and in affording a continuous
opportunity to exercise it."[9]

Beyond being upset at the Supreme Court for in-
truding into what many perceived to be a local matter, most critics of *Miranda* were especially angered
by the Court acting as a type of supralegislature,
coming up with its own set of procedural rules that
all police throughout the nation would be required
to follow. But consistent with its impatience with the
failure of local law enforcement officials and state
legislators to devise their own procedural rules for
eliminating illegally coerced confessions, the Court
was convinced of the necessity of becoming a policy
formulator in the field of criminal justice. The Court
itself was somewhat divided on this question, yet despite the fact that *Miranda* was such a closely con-
tested 5-4 decision, it has never been directly
overruled in the ensuing thirty years, even though
the Court experienced radical changes in personnel.
In his perceptive volume on the *Miranda* decision
and its aftermath, Otis Stephens writes that regardless of the unpopularity of the decision, the Supreme
Court in *Miranda*

> *served to direct national attention to serious
> problems of government and politics that
> might otherwise go unattended. If its contro-
> versial attempt to upgrade interrogation
> practices has increased public and profession-
> al awareness of a weak point in the system,
> the Court's effort will not have been altogether
> pointless. Current emphasis on the greater
> professionalization of law enforcement may,
> in fact, owe much to Supreme Court involve-*

*ment in the confession field. Whatever policy
alternatives they choose in the future, the justices can be expected to continue grappling
with many unresolved questions of confession
admissibility. It seems likely, however, that
the Court will defer to other agencies of government in the formulation of additional
guidelines for police interrogation.*[10]

As a common-law nation that depends upon precedents rather than codified laws, an appellate decision, even from a court as important as the U.S.
Supreme Court, may be of marginal significance.
This is because its future application by other courts
in subsequent cases can often be evaded through
narrow interpretation or by distinguishing it from
the earlier precedent. Because no two cases are ever
exactly the same and because common law only en-
courages rather than requires the use of precedent,
the process of evading an unpopular decision is not
very difficult. Chief Justice Warren understood this
process all too well, especially because many of his
earlier cases that dealt with both the civil rights
field and the rights of persons accused of crimes had
been unpopular and had been undermined in subsequent decisions. Because he felt so strongly about
the abuses of police officers during station house interrogations and realized the weaknesses of the
common-law system, Warren thought that his decision in *Miranda* must provide a formal set of guidelines that could not be easily circumvented. Thus the
decision adopted the unusual strategy of providing
police officers with specific requirements that they
must follow after arresting a suspect and taking him
or her into custody, if the product of the interrogation is to be legally admissible. These rules, which
were soon printed on cards and read by policemen to

all suspects, instruct defendants as to their Fifth and Sixth Amendment rights: the right to remain silent because anything they say can be held against them and the right to an attorney, and if the defendant is indigent, the state will provide one for him or her.

In the previous chapter's examination of the impact of the *Miranda* decision and the degree of compliance, it was obvious that many subsequent Supreme Court decisions attempted to minimize or restrict the implications of the decision. Nevertheless, no case has tampered with the essence of the decision: the specific requirements necessary for guaranteeing the admissibility of confessions. These guidelines have survived, in large part because of their clarity and codelike certainty.

Although critics may believe that the Supreme Court in *Miranda* swung too far in helping criminals avoid successful prosecution, the decision continues to serve for most as a pinnacle of the due process revolution. It is a decision that marks the highwater mark of the Warren Court's efforts to breathe life into the due process rights of all Americans. David Simon is a reporter whose research on Baltimore homicide detectives allowed him to observe countless police interrogations for over a year. In his prize-winning book based on this unforgettable experience, Simon captures the essence of *Miranda's* impact on the policeman's ability to obtain confessions by writing that:

> Miranda *is, on paper, a noble gesture which declares that constitutional rights extend not only to the public forum of courts, but to the private confines of the police station as well.* Miranda *and its accompanying decisions established a uniform concept of a criminal de-*

*fendant's rights and effectively ended the use
of violence and the most blatant kind of physical intimidation in interrogations. That, of
course, was a blessing.*[11]

The *Miranda* decision has obviously aroused strong
sentiments from both its supporters and critics. To a
large measure one's evaluation of the opinion will be
heavily influenced by attitudes toward federalism,
defendants' rights, societal security, states' rights,
and other related constitutional and ideological
predilections. As a final comment, I believe the *Miranda* decision should be viewed the way author
Liva Baker has placed it in its historical context.
She explains:

Miranda *was a statement of aspiration. It
had been 700 years in the writing, counting
only from Magna Carta. John Lilburne [a
seventeenth-century English political agita-
tor] was a minor character in it; the ghostly
figures of Izell Chambers and Clarence Earl
Gideon and Danny Escobedo marched between the lines. Abe Fortas, who had suggest-
ed at oral argument that the cases of these
convicted rapists and murderers and holdup
men were not just isolated cases but held
some meaning for political history, said some
years later about* Miranda: *"[S]omeday, in a
better world, it may be a predicate for a ruling that confessions obtained by police or
prosecutor, from a person in custody, are inadmissible if taken in the absence of counsel."
More than looking toward only some more
civilized rule of evidence, however, the decision by the United States Supreme Court in
the case of Ernest Miranda looked toward
some higher degree of civilization itself.*[12]

DEFENDANT	LOCATION

SPECIFIC WARNING REGARDING INTERROGATIONS

1. YOU HAVE THE RIGHT TO REMAIN SILENT.

2. ANYTHING YOU SAY CAN AND WILL BE USED AGAINST YOU IN A COURT OF LAW.

3. YOU HAVE THE RIGHT TO TALK TO A LAWYER AND HAVE HIM PRESENT WITH YOU WHILE YOU ARE BEING QUESTIONED.

4. IF YOU CANNOT AFFORD TO HIRE A LAWYER ONE WILL BE APPOINTED TO REPRESENT YOU BEFORE ANY QUESTIONING, IF YOU WISH ONE.

SIGNATURE OF DEFENDANT	DATE
WITNESS	TIME

☐ REFUSED SIGNATURE   SAN FRANCISCO POLICE DEPARTMENT   PR.9.1.4

The San Francisco Police Department uses this form to make sure that suspects are informed of their Miranda *rights. The procedures mandated by* Miranda *help guarantee that police do not deny suspects their constitutional rights and that courts can trust that confessions and other statements made by suspects are voluntary.*

SOURCE NOTES

CHAPTER 1
1. Liva Baker, *Miranda: Crime. Law and Politics*, (New York: Atheneum, 1983), 358.
2. *Ibid.*, 13.
3. *Ibid.*, 19.
4. *Ibid.*
5. *Ibid.*, 22.

CHAPTER 2
1. *Arizona v. Miranda*, 98 Arizona 18 (1965), p. 35
2. *Ibid.,* 32–37.
3. Baker, 59.
4. *Ibid.*, 60.
5. David O'Brien, *Storm Center* (New York: Norton, 1993), 248.
6. Fred Graham, *The Due Process Revolution* (New York: Hayden Book Co., 1970), 155.

CHAPTER 3
1. Frances Allen, "The Supreme Court and State Criminal Justice," *Wayne Law Review* 4 (1957), 191.
2. Craig N. Bradley, *The Failure of the Criminal Pro-*

cedure Revolution (Philadelphia: University of Pennsylvania Press, 1993), 1.

3. Lawrence S. Wrightsman and Saul M. Kassin, *Confessions in the Courtroom* (Newbury Park, CA: Sage Publications, 1993), 60.

4. *Ibid.*, 61.

5. J. H. Wigmore, *Evidence in Trials at Common Law*, vol. 3 (Boston: Little, Brown, 1970), 294.

6. Wrightsman and Kassin, 21.

7. Leonard Levy, *Origins of the Fifth Amendment* (Oxford: Oxford University Press, 1968), ix.

8. Stephen Markham. "*Miranda v. Arizona*: A Historical Perspective," *American Criminal Law Review* 24/2 (1987), 196

9. Levy, 196.

10. Markham, 196.

11. Fred Inbau and J. E. Reid, *Criminal Interrogation and Confessions* (Baltimore: Williams and Wilkins, 1962).

12. Jack C. Plano and Milton Greenberg, *The American Political Dictionary*, 6th ed. (New York: Holt, Rhinehart, and Winston, 1982), 122.

13. 110 U.S. 516 (1884).

14. 302 U.S. 319 (1937), 325.

15. 211 U.S. 78 (1908).

16. Laurence Friedman, *Crime and Punishment in American History* (New York: Basic Books, 1993), 361.

CHAPTER 4

1. Bradley, 3.

2. Anthony Lewis, *Gideon's Trumpet* (New York: Random House, 1967), 84.

3. *Ibid.*

4. Otis Stephens, *The Supreme Court and Confessions of Guilt* (Knoxville: Univ. of Tennessee Press, 1973), 203.

5. *Ibid.*

6. Markham, 198.

7. Henry Foster, "Confessions and the Station House Syndrome," 18/2 & 3 *DePaul Law Review* 695 (Summer, 1969).

8. 110 U.S. 574 at 584–85 (1884).

9. 168 U.S 532 at 561 (1897).

10. 318 U.S. 332 at 343–44 (1943).

11. Markham, 201.

12. 297 U.S. 278 at 285 (1935).

13. *Ibid.*, 278–79.

14. 309 U.S. 227 at 239–40 (1940).

15. Monrad Paulsen, "The Fourteenth Amendment and the Third Degree," 6 *Stanford Law Review* (1954), 421.

16. Markham, 205.

17. 378 U.S. 1 (1964).

18. *Crooker v. California* 357 U.S. 433 (1958) and *Spano v. N.Y* 360 U.S. 315 (1959).

19. Graham, 163.

20. 378 U.S. 478 at 491 (1964).

21. "How Supreme Court Ruling Puts Straight Jacket on Police," *Chicago Tribune* (August 11, 1964), 27.

22. Graham, 155

23. *Ibid.*, 170.

CHAPTER 5

1. Charles Evans Hughes, *The Supreme Court of the United States* (New York: Columbia University Press, 1928), 61.

2. William Brennan, quoted in "Report of the Commission on Revision of the Federal Court Appellate System," *Structure and Internal Procedures: Recommendations for Change*, 67 Federal Rules and Decisions 195 (1975), 254.

3. Lewis Powell, Remarks at Fifth Circuit Judicial Conference, May 27, 1974, quoted in R. Stern and E. Gressman, *Supreme Court Practice* (Washington, D.C.: BNA, 1978), 732.

4. *Vignera v. NY* 384 U.S. 436 (1966); *Westover v. U.S.* 384 U.S. 436 (1966); and *California v. Stewart* 384 U.S. 436 (1966).
5. Graham, 176–77.
6. *Ibid.*, 129..
7. *Ibid.*, 130.
8. *Ibid.*, 177.
9. O'Brien, 275.
10. 384 U.S. 436 (1966), 439.
11. *Ibid.*, 455.
12. *Ibid.*, 439.
13. *Ibid.*, 496.
14. *Ibid.*, 458.
15. *Ibid.*, 459.
16. 277 U.S. 438 at 468 (1928)
17. Graham, 193.
18. *Ibid.*
19. 384 U.S. 436 at 504.
20. *Ibid.*, 517.
21. *Ibid.*, 526.
22. Markham, 195.
23. Stephen Schulhofer, "Reconsidering Miranda," 54 *University of Chicago Law Review* (1987) 45 .

CHAPTER 6
1. Baker, 180.
2. *Ibid.*
3. *Ibid.*, 358.
4. 384 U.S. 719 (1966).
5. *Ibid.*
6. Remarks of Senator Sam Ervin (N.C.), 112 *Congressional Record* (August 29, 1966), 21040.
7. Baker, 165.
8. *Ibid.*, 171.
9. *Ibid.*, 172.
10. Wrightsman and Kassin, 48.
11. Vincent Blasi, ed., *The Burger Court: The*

Counter-Revolution That Wasn't (New Haven: Yale University Press, 1983), 83.

12. Jerrold Israel, "Criminal Procedure, the Burger Court, and the Legacy of the Warren Court," 75 *Michigan Law Review* (1977), 1379.

13. 429 U.S. 492 (1977).

14. Robert Jacob, "The State of Miranda," 21/1 *Trial* (1985), 44.

15. Fred Cohen, "Miranda and Police Interrogation: A Comment on Illinois v. Perkins," 26/6 *Criminal Law Bulletin* (1990), 546.

CHAPTER 7

1. "Interrogations in New Haven: The Impact of Miranda," 76 *Yale Law Review* (1967), 1585.

2. *Ibid.*, 1611.

3. Stephens, 170.

4. Richard Medalic, Paul Alexander, and Leonard Zeitz, "Custodial Police Interrogation in Our Nation's Capital," 66 *Michigan Law Review* (1968), 1347.

5. *Ibid.*, 1348.

6. *Ibid.*, 1391.

7. Lawrence Leiken, "Police Interrogation in Colorado: The Implementation of Miranda," 47 *Denver Law Journal* 48 (1970).

8. Arthur Goldberg, *Equal Justice* (Evanston: Northwestern Univ, Press, 1971), 19.

9. *Miranda v. Arizona* 384 U.S. 436 at 490 (1966).

10. Stephens, 206.

11. David Simon, *Homicide* (Boston: Houghton, Mifflin, 1991), 199.

12. Baker, 383.

FOR FURTHER READING

The most detailed and comprehensive account of the *Miranda v. Arizona* decision is *Miranda: Crime, Law and Politics* (New York: Atheneum, 1983) by Lina Baker. It is an extremely readable analysis of not only the case but its political and legal consequences in the succeeding decades. For an excellent overview of the Supreme Court's operation and procedures, as well as the entire federal judicial system, David O'Brien's *Storm Center: The Supreme Court in American Politics* (New York: Norton and Company, 1996, 4th Edition) is highly recommended.

An excellent historical treatment of confessions is offered by Lawrence S. Wrightsman and Saul Kassin in *Confessions in the Courtroom* (Newbury Park, CA: Sage Publications, 1993). Otis Stephen's *The Supreme Court and Confessions of Guilt* (Knoxville: Univ. of Tennessee Press, 1973) provides a readable legalistic and scientific analysis of the case. Because *Miranda* is also concerned with the right to counsel issue, Anthony Lewis's *Gideon's Trumpet* (New York: Random House, 1967) is must reading.

Those wishing to learn more about Chief Justice Earl Warren, author of the majority opinion and leader of the due process revolution, are encouraged to read Bernard Schwartz's *Super Chief: Earl Warren and His Supreme Court—A Judicial Biography* (New York: New York University Press, 1983). Finally, Richard Harris's *Freedom Spent* (Boston: Little, Brown, 1976) illustrates how difficult it can be to exercise one's constitutional rights fully.

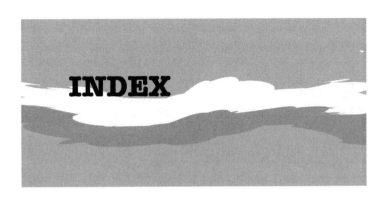

INDEX

ABOUT THE AUTHOR

Paul B. Wice teaches political science at Drew University in Madison, New Jersey. He has received awards for excellence in teaching from the New Jersey Department of Higher Education and Drew University. Professor Wice has been a visiting scholar at the U.S. Department of Justice and the New Jersey Supreme Court. He is the author of seven books on criminal law and *Gideon v. Wainwright and the Right to Counsel*, another title in Franklin Watts's Historic Supreme Court Cases series.